A Messed-Up Ride or a Dressed-Up Walk

A Messed-Up Ride or a Dressed-Up Walk

A Stirring Autobiography of
Hope for the City,
Love for God, and a Faith
That Stays the Course

by Jerald January
with Steve Wamberg

ZondervanPublishingHouse
Grand Rapids, Michigan

A Division of HarperCollins*Publishers*

A MESSED-UP RIDE OR A DRESSED-UP WALK
Copyright © 1994 by Jerald January with Steve Wamberg

For more information please write:
Zondervan Publishing House
Grand Rapids, Michigan 49530

January, Jerald, 1959–
    A messed-up ride or a dressed-up walk : a stirring autobiography
of hope for the city, love for God, and a faith that stays the course /
Jerald January, with Steve Wamberg.
    p.   cm.
    ISBN 0-310-48540-1
    1. January, Jerald, 1956–   . 2. Afro-American Baptists—Clergy—
Biography.   I. Wamberg, Steve.   II. Title.
BX6455.J27A3 1994
277.3'0825'092—dc20   94-27606
    [B]   CIP

All Scripture quotations, unless otherwise indicated, are taken from the
Holy Bible: New International Version®. NIV®. Copyright © 1973, 1978, 1984
by International Bible Society. Used by permission of Zondervan Publishing
House. All rights reserved.

Edited by Lori Walburg
Interior design by Joe Vriend
Cover design by John Lucus
Cover photo by Marcia Ward
African garments provided by Emis African Fashions in Denver, Colorado
Accessories provided by Akente Express in Denver, Colorado

Printed in the United States of America

94 95 96 97 98 99 / DH / 6 5 4 3 2 1

This book is dedicated to my mother,
Hazel Paul-January
I think of you every day
I love you

Contents

Acknowledgments

I WOULD LIKE to thank the following individuals for their part in my journey thus far and the role they played in the inspiration of this book.

My darling wife, Jerra, who has been my constant support and inspiration. My beloved children, Chanè, Craig, Jerald Jr., Charlene, and James, for whom I work every day to leave them a better world. My grandparents Rose and Cary January, for the love you gave me. My father, John January Sr., for the blood that flows through my veins. My brothers John Jr., Jeff, and Keith—you're what true brothers are all about. My little brother Andre, whom I promise I'll never forget (rest in peace). Aunt Nadine, thanks for your everlasting faith in me and your drive for excellence. Aunt Ada, for your example of God's love and for being no respecter of persons. Jerome and Audrey Dandridge, the best in-laws in the world. All my uncles, aunts, cousins, nephews, and nieces, for being yourselves. My best friend and big brother in the faith, Donald Williams, for always being a true friend. My capable assistant, Doris Holloway, for all her hard work. All the people who have had an everlasting impact on my life, including these few: Mark and Ella Pollard, Larry and Cassandra Norton, James Newby, C. R. Phillips, Flora Jackson, Frank Jackson, Gary and Sherri Brown, the Cornerstone Church Family, Mike and Sharon Johnson, Dave Pyle, Samuel Wright, John Selman, Roger Cross, Sam Hooks, Mary Paul,

John Lawrence, James Slappy, Ken Thomas, Claude and Addie Wyatt, Denise Fairfax, and Fred Luthy. Steve Wamberg for his energy, dedication, and immense editing talents in helping me get the words right. The entire Zondervan family for providing the vehicle to tell my story.

Last but always first, I thank Jesus Christ, who is the shepherd who definitely leads me.

Introduction

I WAS BORN in Detroit, Michigan, in December 1956.

My brothers and I were raised by my grandparents on Lawrence Street, just off 12th Street, which is now called Rosa Parks Avenue. You remember Rosa Parks, don't you?

The same month I was born, the Supreme Court ruled against the Alabama state law that required blacks to sit in the back of public transportation vehicles. Rosa Parks put that law to the test when she refused to move to the rear of a bus on Cleveland Avenue in Montgomery in December 1955. Rosa Parks was supposed to move just because she was black. She was arrested because she didn't.

Martin Luther King led a huge boycott against the Montgomery bus system the following year. The Supreme Court ruling of December 1956 was considered by many to be the first victory for the black civil rights movement.

Rosa Parks started that ball rolling. I grew up about six blocks from her house.

My grandfather had to leave school after the sixth grade to help his family, but he had a lot of street smarts. More than once he told me, "If I had a high school education, I'd have been President of the United States." I have every reason to believe that.

After my freshman year of college at Ferris State, I landed a summer job at the Detroit Zoo. It was quite a distance from home to the zoo, and I had no car.

Granddaddy was a Pontiac Bonneville nut, so if any of us was to get a car with Granddaddy's help, that car was destined to be a Bonneville. Granddaddy gave my brother Johnny a Bonneville. It was an old blue bomb that would not be destroyed. I watched it get hit with a Louisville Slugger once, and the bat left only a small dent in "The Blue Bomb."

Strong cars, those Bonnevilles. The Blue Bomb was so roadworthy that two years of my brother's abuse couldn't put it under. Two years of maintenance neglect and my brother's lead foot hardly slowed it down. Two years of letting the interior fall apart, and still the Bonneville kept on.

Two years had only prepared the Bonneville to be passed on as the family treasure it had become. So when I needed a car for that summer job, Granddaddy suggested that my brother give the Bonneville to me. After all, he had another car by then.

By the time I got it, the Blue Bomb was just plain ugly. It was trashed inside and out. But it ran, so I drove it to work. Understand, there were a lot of nice-looking girls working at the Detroit Zoo that summer. There were a lot of Michigan State guys with great-looking cars there, too. But I had THE BOMB. If I could have had a brand new 1975 Mustang, I could have been the happiest young African American alive. *That* ride was gorgeous, a status symbol—even the *radio* sounded better in a 1975 Mustang.

I remember going home and trying, in my own way, to talk Granddaddy into buying me another car. I worked the image angle with Granddaddy: there I was, a young black man with an Afro, on my way to my sophomore year of college, needing to make a good impression on the young ladies who were laughing at my car. The whole time I was trying to persuade Granddaddy, he was giving me this strange look that just got more intense as I talked.

I did my best pitch and waited for his reply. Finally he said, "Well, boy, a messed-up ride is better than a dressed-up walk."

I never mentioned the Bonneville to Granddaddy again. I understood what my grandfather was saying: Let your pride do what it wants to. You can look great and "dressed-up" and walk to where you need to be, and never get there on time or at all. Or, you can realize that sometimes you're forced to be in circumstances that don't look good to you, but they will get you where you need to be. The ride is "messed-up," but at least you're getting there.

Occasionally, though, it *is* better to have a dressed-up walk. I can't forget what Rosa Parks showed us all. Blacks in Montgomery could have ridden the bus and supported a system that counted them less than human. Instead, they chose to walk to and from work for a full year dressed as domestics, blue-collar workers, and professionals. That dressed-up walk brought a lot of good to the country.

It's a question of timing. We all have a destination we have to reach. If we all have to walk to get there, we may miss destiny. But we can't be taken for a ride that costs us our humanity either.

The circumstances in our culture, our churches, our families, and our careers may not be all we'd like them to be. The key question is this: Are you getting where you need to be at the time God has appointed for you?

From the time I was small till now, I've wondered about my place in society. I've questioned my relationship with the church and the Christian world. I've agonized over my career and my family.

It's taken a while, but I realize I'm getting to where I need to be.

You see, getting there is the goal. So I'll take a messed-up ride if I need to. I'll do a dressed-up walk to bring about God's justice anytime. Because this way, whenever I go forward, it's a testimony to God's goodness.

You'll see why.

Part 1
Early Days

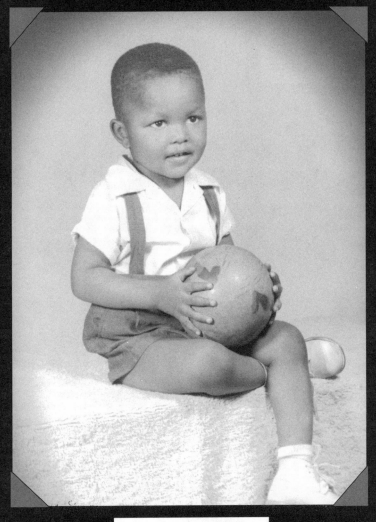

Jerald January—age three

My mom's junior-high school graduation picture.

My father and mother, John and Hazel January, back in the mid-fifties.

1

When Is Mama Coming Home?

Her children arise and call her blessed.
(Proverbs 31:28)

MOST OF MY elementary schoolmates knew me as "the boy without a mother." They were wrong.

My three brothers and I had a mother. Though John, Jeffrey, Keith, and I were raised most of our lives by our grandparents—in fact, we call my father's mother "Mama" to this day—my biological mother was a pretty, round-faced, dimpled black lady by the name of Hazel.

Hazel Louise Marie Paul was born in Almyra, Arkansas, on May 29, 1936. She was murdered on April 28, 1959. I am told my mother loved her middle names and signed her name using both of them. I am also told she loved her sons very much.

My mother's background was typical for the average Negro family of the day. Not long after Hazel was born, her family moved to Stuttgart, a larger town not far from her birthplace. Her father, Lou David Paul, worked in a rice processing plant while her mother, Lily Ada Washington Paul, did domestic work.

My aunt Nadine tells me that she and my mother enjoyed a pleasant childhood. They played jacks together and cut paper dolls out of catalogs. Grandma Lily saved her money to buy Hazel and Nadine nice things like birthstone rings, lockets, and bracelets. The Pauls of Stuttgart were considered a "well-kept" family, and they were respected in the community.

Like most towns in the South of the thirties and forties, Stuttgart was segregated. Black families, regardless of their socioeconomic status, lived in one section of town. The Pauls lived on Porter Street across from the First Baptist Church, and next to a funeral home.

Hazel was a rather quiet child. Some might even describe her as stoic. When my grandparents decided to tell their girls that there was no Santa Claus, Hazel took it in stride, but Nadine wept miserably. And when Hazel was told that her mother, my Grandma Lily, was dying from cancer, she stopped crying on the spot as soon as Nadine came to find out what was the matter.

But don't think for a moment that Hazel Louise Marie Paul had a dreary life. Saturday was movie day in Stuttgart, and the Paul sisters regularly enjoyed the cowboy serials and popular features of the forties and fifties. Sunday was church day, and the Pauls were active in the Baptist church across the street, attending everything from services in the morning to the Baptist Training Union at night. Hazel didn't date much in Stuttgart, but she and Nadine could review the eligible young men of Stuttgart at Friday night football and basketball games. The Pauls of Stuttgart even traveled to visit relatives in Detroit, Chicago, and St. Louis as money allowed. And when she was fourteen, Hazel had the opportunity to take in the Thanksgiving Day football classic at Arkansas State in Pine Bluff.

Still, my mother and her little sister, Nadine, had to grow up quickly when Grandma Lily died on May 27, 1952. Soon after Lily's passing Lou Paul moved to Detroit for work and left Hazel and Nadine in Stuttgart alone in the house, but under the watchful care of relatives and friends. Seven months later, at Christmas time, Hazel decided to close the house in Stuttgart and move to Detroit. She was sixteen and Nadine was fourteen when they boarded the train that took them away from everything they knew.

In Detroit, the girls moved in with their grandparents. Although Northern High School was huge compared to the school they'd left behind, the girls quickly adjusted to their new surroundings. They both excelled in their classes and made many friends. However, the girls felt crowded in their grandparents' house and often talked of getting jobs and moving in together after they graduated from high school.

When Hazel graduated from Northern High in June 1954, she soon landed a good job at a nearby restaurant, and Nadine looked forward to their moving out and enjoying life as single young women. So she and everyone else in the Paul household were shocked when Hazel announced she was in love with John January, and that they intended to be married. Hazel was only eighteen when she married my father in January 1954. My older brother, John Jr., was born a year later. I came along thirteen months later on December 31, 1956, when my mother was twenty years old.

I was only two and a half when my mother was murdered. When my great-grandmother and my brothers Johnny, Jeff, and I heard the shots, we ran into the kitchen. I must have seen her, but my mind blanks out the scene. I do remember running down the hall to our neighbors' apartment and my great-grandmother banging on the door. When the neighbors opened their door, my brothers and I ran into their apartment and ran into a bedroom and jumped up and down on their bed, screaming at the top of our lungs.

Because I was so young when it happened, I didn't know for a long time that my mother had been murdered. My younger brothers and I believed for a while that our mother had died in an accident. I believe my older brother John remembered something, but he didn't talk about it.

What I know about my mother is what I've found out from family members. A lot of it comes from Aunt Nadine. She has said time and again, "Your mother was the strong one. She was always willing to take a chance." And she once told me she'd had a dream the night before my mother died. In her dream Mom was packing her bags. When she was done packing, she kissed us all good-bye and just walked away up into the sky. The next night, my mom was dead—at just twenty-two years old.

My aunt told me that for weeks after my mother was murdered I would stand by the window and ask, "When is Mama coming home? When is Mama coming home?"

It haunts me sometimes that I don't remember my mother better. I know that she was very neat, because I remember lying in my bed and seeing freshly polished shoes lined up from the biggest to the smallest on the windowsill. Sometimes I can remember her warmth or her smile. But these memories come in brief flashes, like a quick cut to a face in a music video.

I spent a great deal of time while I was growing up trying to explain where my mother was. Don't get me wrong; I didn't have to. I never felt ashamed of my grandparents. It's just that I didn't have a young mother like everyone else had. It was normal for other guys not to have a father around, but everyone had a mother.

Except me.

That's the way it seemed. Saying my mom was dead didn't sound right. Deep inside I didn't want anyone to know she was dead. And I was jealous of other kids who had mothers. I couldn't understand why they would complain about their mothers or fight with them. *How can they yell at their mothers?* I wondered. *What's wrong with them? How can they disobey their moms? I just wish mine was around!*

At around age eleven, I found out that my mother had been murdered with a handgun. Before then, as a young boy, I had played with toy guns. But when I found out about her death, I found it difficult to look at or touch a gun, and even the smell and sound of firecrackers bothered me. Nor could I watch movies that portrayed head wounds, especially after I found out that my mother had died from multiple gunshot wounds to the head.

I could bring statistics to bear about the impact of violence on society, but I'd rather let you know where the last thirty-five years of dealing with my mother's death has left me. I pray you never have such an experience, but please know: this thing will always be with me.

Most people didn't notice that Hazel Louise Marie Paul January was murdered. It was just another dead black lady. No headlines in the news, no big deal in Detroit. And since her death, murder has become even more commonplace. We've turned murder into entertainment, and usually the box office blockbusters are those that are the most creative and technically efficient in showing "kills." But by the fake grief of actors in murder scenes, I can tell that they rarely, if ever, have experienced an actual murder. Nothing they could ever do could possibly portray the feelings that attack your heart and mind in the split second you realize someone you love has been murdered.

I've been watching death all my life. It doesn't matter who kills. It doesn't matter if it's a Klan member or a gang member. There will be children, or family, or loved ones who will be alone. People are still dead. The funerals look the same, the hurt feels the same, the shock and loneliness are real.

In my mind, I've never said good-bye to my mother. We didn't even go to her funeral. We were young, and I'm sure our family tried to protect us from the trauma. But even when I finally had the opportunity to visit my mother's grave a few years ago, I didn't get as emotional as I'd imagined I would. The tears didn't come. All that was there was a stone marker and some grass. To me, my mother wasn't there.

I believe it is a great honor for a man or a woman to stand beside the grave or body of their father or mother. To stand tall and strong, and to say, "Thank you."

And "good-bye." I know my belief about this comes from the fact that I wasn't able to say any of those things to my mother. When my grandfather died, I did. But with Mom, I wasn't able to.

People should honor their mothers and fathers. It's like the Scripture says in Exodus 20:12: "Honor your father and your mother, so that you may live long in the land the LORD your God is giving you." Honor them. Every day they come home, every meal they cook, every bed they make, every diaper they change. Every Mother's Day, you have the chance to scramble some eggs and serve her breakfast in bed. You can even send flowers.

Honor them. The opportunities we have to show respect for our parents should never be taken for granted. My mother never came home for me. She never cooked another meal for us. Neither did she polish our shoes again. More importantly, John, Jeffrey, Keith, and I were denied that privilege—too often taken for granted—of receiving the love that can only be offered by a mother. We were cheated out of the special hugs and comforting kisses that only your mother can provide. I suppose the thing that was hardest to realize was the fact that she was just gone. One moment she was with us . . . and then she wasn't.

I believe in heaven. I believe heaven is real and the true home of all those who trust God for salvation.

I really like thinking about heaven being "home." I'm looking forward to going to heaven, because I'm anticipating going home. My Lord will be there, and that alone will make it heaven.

But you know something else? I hope Mom's there, so we can finally be home together.

2
Going Back to Evergreen

Remember the days of old;
consider the generations long past.
Ask your father and he will tell you,
your elders, and they will explain to you.
(Deuteronomy 32:7)

AS I GREW up, my favorite stories were the ones my grandmother would tell from her childhood. "Mama" was the daughter of a Baptist preacher. Reverend Ike Kelly was well known in the parts of Alabama he served. He raised his sons and daughters to pray and believe in God's Word. He gave them a life rich in faith and laughter. Mama talked about her father fondly. As long as I can remember her favorite saying was, "Papa always said to watch as well as pray."

But she had stories to tell about Reverend Kelly's life in the ministry, too. We'd ease ourselves into comfortable positions to listen, and then she'd tell a story like this:

"Because Papa was a preacher, he'd often take me along to the weddings and funerals he performed. Now one of those funerals was for Mr. Jones. Mr. Jones was one of those quiet people in town. Not flashy, not loud, just ordinary. He died in an ordinary way: suddenly at home, presumably from a heart attack.

"In those days, it was the custom to hold a wake for the departed in the living room of his home. Friends and family would all come to the house to view the body and pay respects to the widow. There would be a brief word from the minister, and then the food brought by all the neighbors would be shared.

"That day of Mr. Jones's funeral, his home was so crowded that the children had to be sent outside to look in through the windows. Everything was going as planned. Papa was finished with his message and was closing the service, I recall, when Mr. Jones sat straight up in his casket and opened his eyes like Count Dracula.

"It wasn't an ordinary funeral anymore! People ran around screaming, including the Widow Jones. Some folks dove through the windows of the house to get out of there! But sure enough, there was Mr. Jones with his eyes open, alive and breathing!

"Now Papa explained to us children that Mr. Jones probably had a stroke and his heart rate had been so slow that the town doctor couldn't detect it. He'd just been in a coma, as far as Papa was concerned, and Papa was probably right. But he could never convince me or any other of the kids in town of that.

"Mr. Jones always walked with a limp from then on. Whenever any of the children in town saw the poor man coming they'd run the other way. I heard he died a few years after the funeral I attended with Papa, and that he stayed dead for his second funeral."

It's a true story, and that's probably why it made anyone who heard Mama tell it laugh all the harder.

Nothing brought the stories out of the mouths of my family like the times we spent in Evergreen, Alabama. What in the world is in Evergreen, Alabama? Did a former president live there? Did famous sports heroes hail from this small rural town some thirty-five miles south of Montgomery? Could it be that Evergreen was the site of some important Civil War battle?

Not a chance! So why would I spend valuable time and paper on such an insignificant small town? That's a fair question.

My reasons are purely selfish. Simply stated, my roots are firmly planted in the red clay earth of this out-of-the-way half-dot on the map. My grandparents on my father's side are from

Evergreen, Alabama. Likewise, my mother's folks are from Stuttgart, Arkansas, another small town in the rural South.

I have good reasons for traveling back to these little towns. Most of my life I've learned about the rich heritage of America's immigrants. The ongoing history lessons that stressed to me the strength of every culture but my own always puzzled me. I have no reason to doubt the importance and need for the celebration that speaks to those who came to America from Europe, yet I found myself longing to hear of my own importance and place in history. While African Americans were not exactly invited to this land by Miss Liberty, she indeed has another child in her house.

Roots are very important. In the dictionary, a *root* can be simply defined as "origin." But let's give the word its broader applications: roots also have the ability to nourish and anchor a plant—or a person, for that matter.

There's an old saying: "If you don't know where you came from, you can't know where you're going." It seems that a good deal of the leadership in the United States has very little knowledge of or respect for the history of the land and its laws. We've gone from being a nation that boldly stated "In God We Trust" to being a nation that flippantly asks, "Who is God, anyway?" I think we've forgotten our connection with our roots. The failure to properly honor that connection is at the heart of situations on the evening news—and in our daily lives—that embarrass, confuse, and frighten us. How could such a seemingly great and moral nation fall so far, so fast?

Likewise, when I see such a great genocide being perpetrated on my own people, largely by my own people, that fall is even more evident. How could we survive the hardship of being drafted into slavery just to have so many willingly enlist into the slavery of drugs? How was it that we survived the bondage of one small white substance called cotton just to be enslaved by another small white substance called crack? How could we survive the horrors of lynching only to begin assassinating thousands of our own young, beautiful men and women each year? When did we make the turn from "Say It Loud, 'I'm Black and Proud,'" to hating, dismembering, and destroying our own families over red and blue bandannas?

The reasons are many, I'm sure. I don't claim to have all the answers. But let me suggest one for now: lost roots.

I won't deny that the hardships my people face are myriad. But when haven't we had problems? Who said the odds were now even? For most of our existence in the land of the free and the home of the brave, things have been stacked against us.

Please understand, this is no attempt to cry over spilled milk. I'm not trying to throw an ethnic "pity party," either. It's just a statement of fact: Ever since we've been here, African Americans have usually lacked the adequate power, finances, and other advantages realized by the dominant culture in America.

So when I hear young black men say "You don't know how hard we have it," as though I should be surprised, I immediately wonder what bus they've been riding on. Somehow, some way, many of the generation with whom we now share the land have lost touch with their roots. The origin, anchor, and nourishment that should give them the insight to strive for excellence, the stability to stand through tough times, and the substance to live and give life to their children are missing. While millions of African Americans are "doing the right thing," there is no doubt something has gone terribly wrong.

When I was approached about writing this book, one of the first things I did was to journey back to Evergreen, Alabama. Somehow I knew it was the logical place to start. Since I never really knew my maternal grandparents, my mother's birthplace was not as moving for me as my dad's. Nevertheless, both Evergreen and Stuttgart represent something that many young people today can't fathom.

It is difficult (maybe even impossible) for me to trace my ancestors back to Africa. Alex Haley did it, but I'm not Mr.

Haley. I don't possess his ability, resources, or family records. But I still marvel at the joy and pride millions of Americans, regardless of race, displayed as Alex Haley unraveled the story of his genealogy in *Roots*. I can't describe exactly how I felt as I watched Haley's adaptation of my people on television, but I can tell you it was special.

Understand, there is a feeling of inadequacy when you don't know where you come from. Many adopted individuals long to know their birth parents even if their adoptive parents have been loving and kind. Somehow there is a longing to be connected to the source of our origin. Without it, we feel inadequate. Since most African Americans are not connected to our motherland as many of our fellow countrymen are, we must redefine our roots where we can. For me and millions of others that means going back to some rural town in the South.

After my mother's death, my grandparents adopted my brothers and me. They had already reared three children of their own and had entered into the "empty nest" stage of their marriage. So why in the world would they take in four boys aged three and a half years to two months?

Probably because they were just doing the right thing at a time they were needed. My grandparents loved all their grandchildren, but my brothers and I were their second set of kids. Because of the unfortunate death of our mother we became the fortunate recipients of "old school" parents.

"Old school" simply means the "old way" of doing things. No doubt had my mother lived we would have been reared with love, warmth, and care. Nothing will ever erase the sense of loss I feel for not knowing her. But God in His grace gave us Cary and Rose January—"Granddaddy" and "Mama"—as parents to give us an advantage when the odds were already stacked against us.

Evergreen, Alabama, is a type of motherland that is a source of strength for me. We are all products of our environments. My environment obviously is deeply rooted in inner-city Detroit, but my grandparents never let us forget where they came from. That included the history of Evergreen. It included how and why things were done the way they were in our family. The importance of family and the need for structure and discipline were all parts of the way my grandparents were raised. They were all part of the "old school."

Family prayer was a part of life for us as early as I can remember. We prayed before every meal. We had real reason to thank God, whether the meal was cornbread and beans or fried chicken and yams. Mama reminded us, "A lot of folks ain't got this kind of food to eat. You need to thank the Lord for what you have." That bit of advice has followed me throughout my journey. I've prayed over my meals ever since. Even in restaurants, I pray. (You can never tell who's back there in the kitchen.)

Strong discipline was another reality of the "old school." It was the kind of discipline that is rare today. Yes, we were disciplined for doing wrong. That included spankings (or, as we more tenderly knew them, "whippings"). I won't get into a psychological, intellectual debate about spanking children. It's up to parents to determine how to raise the child God has entrusted to them. I can only testify to the fact that strong discipline worked for my grandparents and father as they raised us. They were very patient and thoughtful in our nurturing. But they believed if talking did no good, the belt would.

You know, they were right. In a community where teen violence and menacing youth were commonplace, the Evergreen way of doing things kept us out of trouble. Not that we weren't tempted often to indulge in everything from mischief to crime. We had no lack of offers and opportunities there! But the words of those who raised us stuck with us, and they were reinforced by the promise of punishment if we disobeyed. Those factors kept us on the straight and narrow. Years later, my brothers and I look back at those days and marvel how we grew up in our neighborhood without getting into trouble.

When we were younger, Granddaddy and Mama would take us to Evergreen during the winter months to live. We'd stay in the old house my folks lived in during their younger family years. My father and his younger brother, Uncle Ulysses, would spend hours telling us about life in that old house and small town.

We had a great time listening to them. We heard a lot about big Friday night games from their high school days. My father was an all-star linebacker for the high school football team. They nicknamed him "Ironman" because he was so tough. I wanted to carry on the family legacy on the football field. I wanted to be just as tough. (Although I played football in high school and college, I don't remember anyone calling me "Ironman." Maybe "Tinman," but not "Ironman.") Uncle Ulysses was the local basketball star known for his great outside shooting. His nickname for life was "Frog." Even we kids called him that.

The stories my father, Frog, and my grandparents shared weren't limited to athletics. They spoke often about the way of life in Evergreen. They told us about the way things were in the thirties, forties, and fifties.

But I just didn't understand many of the stories they told. For example, for years of their lives my grandparents had not been allowed to vote. Even though they had the responsibility of raising a family and bills to pay, they had no say in who would be their President or their county dog catcher. They just had to live with whomever someone else elected into office, and whatever laws were passed.

There were stories of good times, but also stories of fear. To this day I can't imagine having to use a substandard bathroom in a public building. The thought of having to enter a movie house through the alley and then being allowed to sit only in the balcony appalls me.

Everything was separate. Separate and not equal. Separate and second class, and sometimes even third class. From the water fountains to the school buildings . . . separate. Separate isn't so bad if, at least, things are equal. But they were not.

There was always the fear of violence. It wasn't the kind of violence most Americans relate to today. It was the sort that kept you in your place. It was the kind that told you that you were a boy even when you knew you were a man.

Granddaddy would get a strange look on his face whenever we'd watch a television show that depicted a lynching, or other abuse, of blacks in the Deep South. We would ask him, "Why do those people take that?"

His answer was always the same. Granddaddy would simply say, "Because they had to."

My brothers and I were children of the sixties. We grew up with super heroes and Black Panthers. There was absolutely no way anybody could heap that kind of abuse on us. It was hard for us to understand initially that there were indeed times when our father, Uncle Ulysses, or Granddaddy were not the same as Ward Cleaver on television. It was hard to believe that they'd lived through a time when someone could have beaten or killed any one of them, and their family could have done nothing about it. Granddaddy once said, "Only God knows how many colored folks will rise up out of the woods of Alabama on Resurrection Day."

All that said, the thing that still endears Evergreen, Alabama, and all the small towns it represents to me is the strength and character of so many people that came out of them. It's obvious that many of these people had to endure injustice and hardship that is seldom chronicled or appreciated in today's culture. It's also apparent that they never lost their dignity, class, or strength.

They endured hardship and obstacles in hope of a better life for the children that would follow. They believed in family and community. The responsibility for the strength it took to raise children in that climate was shared by the whole town. When one did well, they all did well.

The underlying factor in all of this was an undeniable faith in God. They had faith that the God who had brought us out of the cotton fields was the God who would someday make it better for our children. God was always dealing in equal opportunity. God came to our churches even before there was integration, much less reconciliation.

God took care of us in practical ways, too. Granddaddy said, "When folks were jumping out of windows during the Great Depression, black folks were still eating good." While God was a Sunday-only God for others, He remained an everyday God for the folks in towns like Evergreen. Even those who found themselves out kicking up their heels and tipping back a cold one on Saturday nights could be found in church on Sundays. That was just the way things were.

People knew who God was and what He had done. There was no mistaking it. We didn't have a religious grocery store full of options from which to choose. There were no shaven-head disciples or gurus standing on the side of Evergreen's dirt roads beckoning us to come over and chant. Neither was there time to waste on gods who could not hear. Time was precious and faith was very real. My people weren't important enough for many of the gods of the day. There were those who even believed and preached that we had no souls to save. But God proved Himself to us. Over and over again prayers were answered when all else had failed. When rights were few and opportunities were fewer, God was answering prayer in Evergreen.

Staying connected to that kind of endurance and strength is one of the reasons I keep going back to Evergreen.

The presence of extended family is lacking today. I would never trade my years growing up in a house filled with family. My brothers, father, and grandparents are my strongest and dearest memories of my early years. But I also remember visits from cousins, aunts, and uncles that keep me grounded to this day in that rich red Alabama earth.

My hope for the youth of today is that, somehow, they could be introduced to their roots. Perhaps you know some young people who are rootless. For some inexcusable reason they find themselves in an unforgiving world without the advantage of the anchor roots can provide. Maybe in times gone by rootlessness would have been more tolerable, but not today. The world we live in has storms and turmoil at every turn. There is no "down time," no rest.

The anchor you provide could keep those lives from drifting away. The time you invest can nourish and reconnect a threatened life to its roots. These lost children may never see Evergreen, but they could find life and love through you.

Part 2
School Years

Jerald January, Central High School Class of 1974

My "mama," Rose January, one of the hippest and most loving grandmothers in Detroit.

Sitting in this very spot, my grand-daddy told me, "A messed-up ride is better than a dressed-up walk."

3 Higher Education

It was he who gave some to be ... teachers.
(Ephesians 4:11)

"COULD I TRADE places with Johnny?" I asked. My grandmother and I were returning home from taking my older brother Johnny to his first day of kindergarten.

"Now, Jerald," Mama replied, "you're too young for school right now. But next year you'll be going."

I remember Johnny's first day of school better than my own. Mama, Johnny, and I had walked the nine blocks from our house to get to school. I'd always wondered what was inside that large building on Lawrence Street.

I was awestruck when I looked into Johnny's kindergarten room. I'd never seen anything like it. The place was filled with all kinds of great stuff. There were plenty of new kids I could play with. This room on the basement floor of William H. Peck Elementary School was so bright and cheery that I felt welcomed right away. Why, they even had little chairs for little people like me!

I was totally mystified, then, that Johnny started screaming every time Mama and I tried to leave. For some reason, Johnny wanted no part of this wonderful environment. In fact, he was going crazy at the thought of having to stay.

"Why is Johnny crying?" I asked Mama. "This is a great place."

I could never understand things from Johnny's point of view. He was the oldest. He was the one who got to do everything first. (That also made him the brother who made all the mistakes first, too.) Johnny was always the biggest. Johnny always had the best ideas, too. At least that's what he told us. So if Johnny told us to do something, most times we'd fall into line and do it.

Johnny also got all the new clothes. That was particularly tough on me. I hated being just a year younger than Johnny, because I had to wear his hand-me-downs. It was hard trying to be "together" in your brother's old shirt. Johnny had the gift of wearing the "cool" right out of clothing. It's a good thing he had bad feet that required special shoes. You know the old saying, "You can't know a man until you walk a mile in his shoes," don't you? I, for one, thank God to this day that there were other ways to get to know my big brother.

Because Johnny put up such a fuss that first day of school, his teacher suggested that Mama and I stay for a while until Johnny got used to his class. In fact, Johnny's teacher encouraged me to participate in the class. There were songs, and puppets, and graham crackers, and milk . . . man, I was having a great time!

Johnny seemed to be settling in, so Mama decided to leave. Johnny started crying again, but it wasn't the first time that tears failed to change our grandmother's mind. The curious thing to Mama was that I started crying as we left the school building. Hey, I wanted to *stay* in school!

It was a long year. It was even longer because Johnny really got into kindergarten after the first day. Every afternoon Johnny would come home and brag about all the great stuff he was doing in school. To hear Johnny tell it, school was Disneyland, Tiger Stadium, and McDonald's all rolled up in one convenient package.

My family always stressed the need for a good education. Between their encouragement and Johnny's stories, it's no wonder I wanted to go to school from the time I was four years old. School was that fun place Johnny went to Mondays through

Fridays. School was the place with the toys and puzzles and things.

One year after Johnny's first day of school I finally began the formal educational process, just as Mama had promised. I embarked on a process of discovery, a process of learning. We played new games and worked on fun puzzles. They kept feeding us snacks. This school thing had definite possibilities.

But, alas, as time passed I made an alarming discovery: school was not always going to be like kindergarten.

First grade in Mrs. McFarland's class meant learning the ABCs—in order—and learning to read. It also meant having to print your name. I had to have extra help at home to do that. Writing my name seems so simple today, but for some reason I just didn't get the hang of it when I was six years old.

I clearly remember the day my dad took it upon himself to teach me that task. I was especially having trouble with the letter "J." Dad went over just how to make a readable "J" with me once, twice, ten times, twenty times. I just wasn't getting it. My father was great with us, but he wasn't the most patient man in Detroit. Finally, at the end of his rope, he resolved to get my attention quickly and decisively. Dad's next step in the educational process that day probably wouldn't be endorsed by the National Education Association, but his method of teaching worked on me. My concentration level rose significantly. Suddenly, I had no problem printing my name. Thirty years later, I'm still making good, solid, readable *J*s.

When I was in second grade, our family moved into a house across the street from the school. It was very convenient to live nearby. But second grade also meant handwriting, and I mean cursive, and serious arithmetic. Learning wasn't always fun anymore, as it had been in kindergarten. By the time I was in third grade, I noticed a pattern developing: every year another grade, every day another lesson.

Maybe Johnny had the right idea his first day of school after all, I thought. Where were the graham crackers and milk? Gone!

I'd been tricked. There were no more half-day parties. I'd been in school all day for years now. Gone were the fun-filled mornings of "Captain Kangaroo" and sleeping on the couch after breakfast. Maybe Johnny had yelled so much his first day at Peck Elementary because he had known that school was not always a party. Maybe he'd already been told that once you were in, you couldn't get out for *thirteen years*!

Sometimes I wanted more than anything to skip school and play in the backyard at home with my younger brothers. In those days, though, school was such an important part of the community it was almost a sin to skip class. And our schools were very strict and well run. Each day began with the Pledge of Allegiance and a prayer. Our teachers kept us in line, our hallways were clean, and we even knew the school song. It made such an impression that even today, if I'm hard pressed, I can still sing most of the Peck school song.

We had other traditions that are long since gone. If one of us kids got out of line, or got into a fight, or didn't do assigned homework, we were subject to a paddling. In fact, Peck Elementary had several teachers who were quite skilled as disciplinarians. One of my teachers, Mr. Mells, called his paddle "The Board of Education." The teachers never zapped you more than twice, but the thought of getting whacked was enough to keep us on the straight and narrow.

The school also had regular Bible stories at the end of the day. Attendance was optional, but many children found their way to those sessions.

Even with all that so-called barbaric education and the "politically incorrect" mixture of church and state, we never went to school afraid for our lives. My teachers stayed around after school to make sure we could talk or get any extra help we needed. They didn't seem to fear for their well-being like so many public educators today. And we learned a lot. We weren't just passed from grade to grade. If we failed a class, we had to take it over until we got it right.

Yes, in those days we were segregated. But it didn't seem to matter much to us kids. We occasionally had white or Asian classmates, and they were treated the same as anyone else in school.

The best part of my education, though, was the teachers in the Detroit Public School system. The heroic men and women who were paid to make sure I had the best education possible were both an inspiration and, many times, the cause of perspiration. They had the task of transferring the needed information from the textbook to my brain. They were charged with the unenviable duty to make information that was oftentimes boring into an exciting adventure that justified taking my valuable time.

Granted, there were some things that wouldn't be exciting even if you got James Brown to sing them to the class. However, some teachers really did better with the material than others. I had instructors who made learning akin to watching cement dry in the dark. Don't get me wrong. I'm sure they spent ample time in college receiving the degree and certification necessary to qualify them for their bone-chilling effort to educate the teeming masses of young students they faced. Nevertheless, the manner in which they pursued their professional endeavors left much to be desired. For some reason, they never caught on that they were competing with the likes of comic books, baseball cards, football, and in later life, "Soul Train" and girls.

But then there were the teachers who made school worth the walk there. These individuals took it upon themselves not only to challenge me, but also to intrigue me with the subject matter. Their styles were unique, but the principles behind their methods were much the same. For instance, these teachers were more than willing to go the extra mile to connect with their students. They not only got into our heads, they also got into our lives. They made the subjects they taught enjoyable. They made the information matter to me. I walked away from their classes feeling that I'd really learned something worth knowing, and convinced that I wanted to know what was going to happen the next time their classes met.

I'm sure every school in Detroit had their share of good teachers. In fact, I'm sure every school system in every town and city has teachers who are worth their weight in gold. But I believe that at Peck Elementary, Durfee Junior High, and Central High Schools I was blessed with a combination of instructors dealt to me from on high.

Please understand that I'm not implying that these great teachers shared Jesus with me. As a matter of fact, many of them never even claimed to be Christian. Still, they gave more of themselves than many Christians I met later in life. Perhaps they were simply dedicated to their profession. I can't say for sure. It really doesn't matter to me what individual reasons they had for their commitment to excellence. All I know is they gave of themselves in a way that had a divine impact on my life.

I can't name here all the teachers I admired. But Mrs. McFarland and Mr. Mells from Peck Elementary are definitely on my list. Mr. Reese took special care to encourage me to be proud of who I am. Mr. Alamesee, who preferred to be called Brother Alamesee, was profoundly dedicated both to his students and to our African homeland. Mr. Guip and Mr. Nanstanski were both art teachers who encouraged me to perfect my gifts. But my favorite teacher of all was an old white lady named Miss Jessie Tregier.

Miss Tregier was known far and wide as "The Crazy Lady of the Sixth Grade." Even the bad kids were scared of Miss Tregier. She wore long print dresses that made her look like Granny from "The Beverly Hillbillies," and she even had a voice like Granny's. She ruled her classes with an iron hand, and her students looked like marine platoons on drill when they walked down the hallways on their way to lunch or an assembly.

However, Miss Tregier was best known for The Stick. Some kids believed The Stick was only a wooden pointer. Others would swear that Miss Tregier had several Sticks for different purposes, or that she changed them on different days of the week. I myself had watched Miss Tregier use The Stick like Moses' rod to part the sea of children who were under her charge.

No one I knew wanted to be in Miss Tregier's class. *Nobody.*

I knew I was doomed when I received my class assignment sheet for my last year at Peck Elementary. Miss Tregier was listed as my homeroom teacher. At that moment, I truly believed God and all His friends had sentenced me to the dungeon of Detroit's educational system for some sin I had committed in the fifth grade.

"You've got to get me out of this woman's class," I begged Mama. "She doesn't like colored kids."

The reality, though, was that Miss Tregier loved all the children in her class, and ninety-nine percent of us were black anyway. Fortunately for me, my grandmother ignored my pleas, and I soon resigned myself to the fact that I was stuck with Granny and The Stick for a whole year. Doomed at such a tender age—and to think that just six years before I had been in kindergarten eating graham crackers, enjoying every minute of my educational experience three floors below Miss Tregier's classroom.

Miss Tregier's classroom itself was legendary. The "older classmen" would never tell us what the big deal about her room was, but on the very first day of sixth grade we found out. Miss Tregier was the master of all she surveyed within those classroom walls. That meant every inch of that room had a purpose and a reason for their existence. She quickly listed her rules to us, and they included one of the strangest class setups I had—or have—ever heard: we could go only one way down the aisles in the classroom.

I'm serious. We had one-way aisles. You could only go toward the front of the room from the aisle next to your desk. When you were ready to return to your seat, you had to go around the outside aisle to the back of the room, find the correct aisle, and then go to your seat. No matter what your reason was for going to the front of the room, once you left your seat you went back around the room. One guy named Keith tried going back the wrong way one day. I think he just wanted to try the old lady. Keith made only two or three steps going against the recommended flow of traffic before Miss Tregier clamped down on him like a S.W.A.T. team. She hit his leg so hard with The Stick that The Stick broke apart.

After that, we all understood that Miss Tregier ran a one-way classroom. And that was the Miss Tregier way.

It didn't take Miss Tregier long to learn our names. She was very interested in us and in our likes, dislikes, and aspirations. We were at the beginning of adolescence, and Miss Tregier was the first teacher to talk to us about our futures. Yes, she was very strict and demanding. But she also held lofty expectations of every student. She told us again and again that we could do anything that we put our minds to.

In Miss Tregier's class, there was no room for messy work. Our penmanship had to be good because from her classroom we were going into junior high—and the next step was adulthood. She wanted us to be ready. And she wanted us to be an example for the rest of the school. She wouldn't let us slouch in our chairs or walk with our heads down. She would always call us "beautiful" or "handsome." Before we knew it we were one of a long line of marine platoons Miss Tregier had led down the hallways, and like the marines we were very proud.

Miss Tregier knew the importance of affirming everyone for his or her efforts. Frequently she would drag someone in from the hallway to brag about her students' work. She didn't care if it was the janitor or the principal; she just wanted someone to know how smart we were. In addition, Miss Tregier always made sure the candy jar on her desk was full. She would call us up front after we'd done well on an assignment and allow us to take a piece of candy from the jar. Then she actually let us eat the candy in class! Teachers never let you eat candy in class. But Miss Tregier did.

In Miss Tregier's class we saw a part of her that very few students in the school saw. Not only was Miss Tregier a good teacher, she was also a good person. We were blessed with a bunch of good teachers at Peck Elementary; our principal Mrs. Bailey saw to it that we had good teachers. But Miss Tregier had something special. I couldn't put my finger on it at first. What made her care so much for children who were obviously not from the same background? Why would she take so much extra time with us? How could she put up with the students who hated her guts?

Then one day she said something that gave me the answer to her commitment and style. To the whole class Miss Tregier said, "I pray for all of you every day." The rest of that conversation to the class has long since faded from my memory, but I will always remember the smile on her face and the light in her eyes when she spoke those words to us. The commitment and love she showed us were directly connected to the love and commitment she had for her Lord. Miss Tregier would probably have been a good teacher anyway, but Christ's love shining through her made her my all-time favorite.

During our graduation ceremony from Peck Elementary, Miss Tregier sat on the end of our row. She was as proud of us as our parents were. When the ceremony was over, Miss Tregier hugged everyone and told us she would miss us. Many of my classmates joined me in having our pictures taken with Jessie Tregier, and we wished her a good summer. We knew that she had prepared us well for what would come later in school.

It was quite a long time before I saw Miss Tregier again. I was preparing for college after my last year of high school. Friends from my church invited me to join them for a service held with a very large, mostly suburban congregation located on the outskirts of Detroit. We arrived early for the service and found our seats. As I surveyed the crowd I spotted a little old woman sitting near the back row. She was greeting people as they walked by. One by one the folks would stop and give her hugs and kisses. When I finally had the opportunity for a clear look, I realized it was Miss Tregier.

One of the young ladies in our group was a former Peck Elementary classmate of mine named Jenita. I pointed out Miss Tregier to her, and we decided to make our way over to speak to her. As we got closer I heard people saying, "Praise the Lord, Sister Jessie . . . God bless you, Sister Jessie . . . " When it was our turn to greet Miss Tregier, I asked if she knew who we were. She replied, "Of course I know who you are." To my amazement, she remembered our names. Immediately she inquired about our lives, our families, and our plans for education. Then she turned and began to tell those around us, "These are two of my babies." She seemed just as pleased and excited to see us as we were to see her. We spoke with her a few more moments before we hugged and said our good-byes.

During the service I turned several times to look at Miss Tregier. The last time I turned, during a time of praise, I noticed her lifting those wrinkled hands to God. She praised Him in a way that openly displayed great love and admiration. That same love had motivated Miss Tregier to teach us and pray for us every day. Now when I think of her, I remember her not only walking down the classroom aisle with one of those old print dresses almost touching the floor, I also see her with arms lifted to the Lord she loved so dearly.

I'm sure that in the twenty years since I saw her last, Jessie Tregier has gone on to be with her Savior. She is probably one of the loudest souls worshiping God around His throne. But somehow I believe that Miss Tregier has also figured out a way to tell the dear souls gathered there about her students. She's probably told them how the Father worked it out for her to work at a school on the west side of Detroit. She's saying, "My last school was in a tough neighborhood in the inner city. In that school, I taught little black boys and girls who were my babies.

"Many of those children came into my class with little hope or self-esteem," I imagine Miss Tregier telling the heavenly hosts. "But when they left, they weren't the same."

The same red and gold brick building where Jessie Tregier taught and gave her students all the love and attention she could is now abandoned and decaying. But because she gave us a higher education about who God was making us to be, Miss Tregier's craftsmanship would never be contained by four walls.

Maybe God has placed you in a position to teach or influence a young person. You may never know what effect your words, instruction, or just plain love could have on their lives.

I'm sure Miss Tregier never knew what those days in her classroom ultimately meant to me.

4 Try Me First

*Taste and see that the LORD is good;
blessed is the man who takes refuge in him.
(Psalm 34:8)*

GROWING UP IN Detroit in the sixties was a soulful experience.

Detroit had its own identity that could be seen and heard every day and night. Our greatest claim to fame, in my opinion, had to be "The Motown Sound." Every day on almost every radio you would hear music that made you move. The Supremes, Smokey Robinson and the Miracles, and the Four Tops always seemed to have a hit. But my favorite group was the Temptations. I know that sounds like an odd choice for an ordained minister, but to this day when I hear David Ruffin or Eddie Kendricks leading out on a song, it's a pure spiritual experience. Fortunately for me, my father loved their music too. So when he'd go buy the latest Temptations record, we'd play it to death while he was at work.

We lived on the west side of Detroit. Most of my young life was spent in a two-family flat on Lawrence between 12th and Woodrow Wilson streets. I lived in the first floor flat with my grandparents, father, and three brothers. My Uncle Frog and Aunt Ada lived upstairs with their six children. Our neighbors simply called it the January House. Neighborhood legend had it that there were thirty kids living in our house. Actually, there were only ten of us there. But it sure helped in our neighborhood when people thought you had twenty-nine brothers!

Downtown Detroit in those days was a seriously happening

place. The streets and stores were always full. J. L. Hudson's, Woolworth's, and dozens of other retailers kept the shopping exciting. Kresge's had the best buttered popcorn in the world. Mama would take us on the bus on Saturdays to spend most of the day looking for bargains. We had great movie theaters in those days, too. The Fox and The Palms always had the latest Frankenstein or Dracula movies.

Like the song says, "everything must change," and by the late 1960s Detroit was in the throes of race riots. At first the riots were sort of exciting. Sirens blew, and people rushed to and fro. But as the riots grew worse, the rioters began to burn down a good portion of the retail business in our neighborhood, along with many apartment buildings. Day after day the news reported the casualties; the number of dead, the damage costs, and all the rest that goes with a riot.

The problem was that this wasn't just on television. This was our city. This was my neighborhood on the TV screen, not some rice paddy in Vietnam. This was where I was growing up. When you're eleven years old, adults don't take time to explain everything to you. They just told us to stay away from the windows and not to play in the backyard anymore.

I disobeyed my folks once during that time. Instead of staying inside the house, like I was supposed to, I snuck onto the back upstairs porch to look around. At that moment, I saw a white National Guardsman walking past. I must have startled him, because when he saw me he immediately pointed his rifle at me. I couldn't move. I was so scared my heart pounded like a jackhammer.

To my dying day, I will never forget the look in his eyes. He looked as scared as I was. Neither of us could relate to the other, but at that moment, we almost became a part of each other's world forever.

The late sixties brought change to many things—too many, perhaps. The assassination of Dr. Martin Luther King seemed to take the life out of whole communities. The death of Senator

Robert Kennedy seemed to mark the end of a very innocent time I call "The Black and White Age." Until 1968, everything seemed to reflect life as we saw it on our old television. Things were black and white and all fuzzy, but there was always a chance that things would get better. We really believed that we would overcome. Surely someone would come along and make the picture clear and sharp and colorful.

By the time the seventies came, television as well as movies was in color, but they weren't any better. *Frankenstein* and *Dracula* gave way to *Superfly* and *Willie Dynamite*. The Fox and The Palms featured slick stories with funky music and urban warriors that got the women and killed everyone else. At first I loved seeing so many black stars on the movie screen. God knows that out of the hours I spent watching television and movies, I had seen only rare glimpses of someone black, unless they were shining shoes or serving dinner. Up to that point I had never even watched a black couple kiss on screen. It made me think there was something wrong with us. Occasionally, you could see a black policeman heroically shooting other blacks on TV dramas. Progressive shows might even feature a black villain, usually a pimp. But what about an ordinary brother just taking care of his family? I guess they couldn't find anyone to play him. Maybe it was impossible to write funky music for that kind of show.

Things were changing all right. Even David Ruffin left the Temptations. I was changing too.

My brothers started a singing group called "The Jacks of Soul" in the early seventies. Their manager, Jack Starks, was very energetic and had The Jacks of Soul on the way to stardom. Due to my "brotherly connection," I played the congas in the band for a while. But music just wasn't my life's calling.

While The Jacks pursued music, I pursued art. As my talent began to bloom, I became convinced that I'd found my life's work. People referred their friends and family members to me for portraits. I sometimes made money doing my art, and I felt an incredible satisfaction while I drew.

But I knew art alone would never be enough to make me happy. I spent hours thinking about what a perfect world, or even some perfect thing, would be like. Even with all the love and support my family offered, I found myself dissatisfied with life—and my dissatisfaction only seemed to get worse. While my brothers had their music and the satisfaction it brought, I had nothing to give me the sense of belonging or peace I was searching for.

By the time I was sixteen I was the veteran of a few relationships with girlfriends. I'd never had any "serious" go-rounds, though. I was never a big one with the ladies. Not that I didn't want to be—I was your average African American teenage male with all the desires deemed necessary to be labeled as such. My big handicap was being so shy that I found talking to girls extremely difficult. Young ladies were like an unknown planet to me. Since there were no girls in my immediate family, I never developed the skills necessary to carry on a decent conversation with them. I had no problem cracking jokes around girls. It was just the serious talk I couldn't handle. As a matter of fact, if I was walking down the street and saw more than one girl walking toward me, I'd cross to the other side of the street almost every time.

There were occasions, of course, when I would make specific plans to speak to a certain girl during class. I planned what I wanted to say. I practiced every clever line in my mind on the way to school. I developed different answers to respond to any reply I imagined that girl might give. I dressed for success in the perfect shirt coordinated with the right pants. I shaped my Afro just right and made it gleam with extra hair spray. I was ready like Freddy.

Then reality would strike. I'd see her standing right in front of me. In the more successful encounters, I'd freeze with my mouth open and say nothing at all. When I was less fortunate,

I'd speak and say totally stupid things. Then the girl would laugh and say, "Oh, Jerald, you're so funny!"

The problem was I wasn't trying to be funny.

On the way home I'd replay those scenes over and over in my mind. I could never quite figure out what the problem was with me. But I knew that using the word "uh" as the basis of communication wasn't working.

Finally, something happened that changed my young non-love life forever. Her name was Denise. It was love at first sight—for me, at least. I was on my way to dress for a football game against a rival school. I had just left my locker and was proceeding down the hall toward the gym. As I passed classroom after classroom, I happened to glance into one—and there she was. She was sitting in a small group. I was stunned. I nearly gave myself whiplash stopping for a better look. I'd never seen her before. I didn't know her name.

Who is this girl? What is this group? Who are these people? The thoughts were coming a mile a minute, but I had to go to the locker room and get dressed. Even during the game I thought about her. (Of course, I had plenty of time on the bench to think.) I didn't care whether we won or lost; I just wanted to know who this girl was.

The following Monday I spoke to the teacher who conducted the meeting in which I saw the girl. With my concerned face intact—the one that makes others feel that you really care about their agenda—I asked what the meeting was about. He informed me that it was the Afro History Club, that it met every week, that he was the supervisor, and that it was important for young blacks to know the history of their people.

At that time I didn't care much about the history of my people. I just wanted to know the history of that girl. So I promised to come to the next meeting to be enlightened.

But then I realized the group met at the same time as our next football game. Football or destiny? What would it be? I had a choice to make, and I made it.

At 3:15 P.M. the following Friday I found myself engrossed in an exciting discussion about Nat Turner and other significant heroes of the past. (Who would ever think that good old Nat could hold the key to my love life?) And there she was: my "first love," Denise. She'd just transferred from another high school and was very impressed with my concern for African-American history and the brothers and sisters that had gone on before us. Denise was even more impressed that I'd skip a football game after a full week's practice in order to gain more insight into my heritage.

Yeah, that was me all right: Mr. Afro History. Don't get me wrong; I was very grateful for all the great things my forefathers had done. But I wasn't about to tell Denise I was there more to find out about a current-day sister than to study Sister Harriet Tubman.

One day as I walked Denise to the bus stop, we stopped at the store to pick up some snacks. I took the opportunity to give her a little lapel pin I'd picked up for her downtown. She stunned me by planting a kiss on my lips.

It was my first real kiss from a girl, and I wasn't ready for it. It seemed like no big deal for her, but it was for me. We eventually became very close. We even shared a locker for a few months, a sign of true love if ever there was one. It was love just like the "happily ever after" kind of love in black-and-white movies.

On one occasion when Denise and I were on the phone she said, "Talk to me, Jerald." That seemed like a fair enough request, and I knew exactly the kind of talk she wanted to hear. But I couldn't find the words to say what was in my heart.

Soon after that listless conversation, Denise lowered the boom and presented me with my walking papers. I wasn't her type. The dream lover she was looking for attended the Catholic high school down the street. Denise closed our talk that day with the classic high school breakup line, "We can always be friends."

Yeah, right. My brother Jeff started calling me "Father Flanagan, the friend of every girl." I'd found out that what they said about love was true. Love really does hurt, and the good guy doesn't always get the girl. Often, they just become friends.

Boy, was I heartbroken. Even with Denise, I just couldn't generate the kind of conversation girls liked.

In those days, "rap" simply meant conversation. Girls of the seventies really liked smooth "rap." Now, my brother John could talk to any girl. Rapping seemed like a gift to that guy. So one day I said to John, "Teach me how to rap."

John had it too easy. He didn't understand my situation. He answered, "All you have to do is just open your mouth and talk."

I knew that wasn't true. My history of conversations featuring the word *uh* was proof.

The months went by. The hole I found myself in seemed to get deeper and deeper. The things that had once brought me joy were no longer fulfilling. My walks downtown seemed endless. The records that had given me solace seemed much shorter.

There were days I'd go to the movies alone. I'd buy a large buttered popcorn and a soda and sit in the theater waiting for Hollywood to pull me out of my funk. It didn't work. Nothing was working anymore.

I don't believe my family had any idea how depressed I'd become. I found myself thinking about my mother more. Surely if Mom were around she would help me. Mom would know what was wrong with me. Yeah, Mom was the answer. But she was gone. She was never coming back. What was I going to do?

While all those thoughts and feelings simmered inside me, Christmas rolled around again. Let me tell you, Detroit can be real nasty in December. For starters, it's cold and gray. Severe depression only adds to the effect, and at sixteen you really don't know what to do to get help. I felt really stupid about not being able to control what I was going through, so I held it all in.

By the time Christmas Eve came I couldn't take it anymore.

The wind seemed colder, the snow was falling harder, and I felt very alone. I made my decision.

Even then I knew life itself was very precious and should be cherished. But I'd come to the conclusion that Jerald January's life was no longer worth living. On what should have been an evening of expectation and excitement, I planned to take my own life.

I know that suicide is one of the leading causes of death among teens today. The pressures that face many of today's youth are monumental and can seem unbearable. Many choose death as the way out, as a door that should lead to rest. I can relate to that hurt. I have experienced the utter sense of hopelessness, and I know there are times in a young life when the world we live in seems so disappointing you think you want to leave it.

I planned my suicide carefully. I waited until nine o'clock Christmas Eve to go into the bathroom, where I knew I'd find the red pills to swallow. At that time in the evening, my grandmother was the only one around. I was sure she wouldn't find me until it was too late.

I wonder now how my grandmother would have been affected if she had found me dead that night. That Christmas Eve, though, the thought never crossed my mind. All I was thinking about was myself. It was some time later before I realized just how selfish suicide was. I was so concerned about my own hurt that no one else really mattered. *Hey, I'm just another black teenager that no one even knows is alive,* I convinced myself.

You must understand, I had to be very desperate even to entertain the thought of killing myself. I don't like pain at all. I'm allergic to pain. But I believed that the pain I felt inside was far greater than the pain I'd go through in dying.

Once I'd shut the bathroom door behind me, I took a final look into the old mirror directly over the sink. I opened the medicine cabinet and grabbed the bottle of pills I knew would be there. They were one of Granddaddy's prescriptions—medicine to him, but poison in the amount I was about to swallow.

I sat down on the floor and leaned back against the bathtub. As I opened the bottle and poured the pills on the floor, I convinced myself one last time: "This is the right thing to do."

I picked up a handful of pills to pop in my mouth. At that instant, I heard three words that would change my life forever.

"Try me first."

I jumped to my feet. *Who was that?* The voice was quiet, yet stern. It was definitely a man. But who?

I knew my grandmother was in the house, but it wasn't her voice. Who was it, then? Was it a hallucination? If it was, it wasn't induced by the pills. They were still in my hand and on the floor.

God. It had to be God, I thought nervously. *Maybe I'm going crazy, but maybe it was God. Why wouldn't I be crazy, anyway? Crazy people kill themselves, right?*

All I knew at that moment was that I had to get out of the bathroom. I quickly scooped the pills back into the bottle and carefully placed the bottle back into the medicine cabinet. I hurried out the bathroom door and surveyed the house.

My grandmother was still sitting on the living room couch. No one else was home.

I began thinking seriously that I could have heard God's voice. Maybe He wanted me to try Him. Sure, I'd been to church enough. My grandmother always needed someone to walk home with her after church, so I'd volunteer to go with her. The music at church was pretty good. Besides, there were a lot of cute girls all decked out in their Sunday best there. Even the sermons were useful in their own way; since they really never made much sense to me, I never stayed awake to hear one all the way through. I really believed, though, that I got my best sleep in church. There was no sleep like church sleep.

Even on the Sundays I'd pass on church to stay home and watch football, I'd always take time out to read at least one verse of Scripture. So maybe it shouldn't have surprised me that God would talk to me. God and I had an understanding, after all. At least I thought we did.

My mind was going a thousand miles a minute. I went to my bedroom and threw myself across the bed. I just wanted to get to the next day, so my response to God was simple.

"If this is really You, God, let me fall asleep," I whispered. "I don't know what I'll do if I stay awake."

All I remember after that is opening my eyes on Christmas morning. I don't remember getting sleepy. I don't remember falling asleep. It seemed I just closed my eyes and opened them, and it was morning.

It was Christmas morning 1973, in fact. Gifts were not on my mind when I awoke. I washed up and walked over to the church I'd been to many times with my grandmother. New Mount Zion Missionary Baptist Church on Elmhurst Street was holding its traditional Christmas service. It was the first time I'd ever gone to New Mount Zion by myself. But after my experience the night before, it seemed to me that I had to be there.

The crowd that morning was sparse. The building that houses New Mount Zion could easily hold several hundred people, but that day there were only fifty people in attendance. To me, it wouldn't have mattered if only five people were there—I just needed to be among them.

The Reverend James Newby, pastor of New Mount Zion, spoke that morning about "God's Gift." For the first time I heard a sermon all the way through. Pastor Newby's message was so clear to me. Everything he said made sense. I found myself wondering, *Why didn't I understand it this way before?*

When the altar call was given, I suddenly found myself standing on my feet. I looked at the aisle. It seemed twenty feet wide that morning. I stepped out and started walking. I wanted to meet the Lord for myself, on His terms. I'd finally understood how important God's gift, Jesus Christ, was to me.

When I made it to the front, Pastor Newby prayed with me and for me. I could feel a load lifting from my shoulders.

Then Pastor Newby asked, "Do you have any special requests?"

"I get bored easily," I replied. "I just don't want to get bored with church."

I'm not sure to this day what Pastor Newby thought of my response, but I do remember his prayer for me. "God, reveal Yourself in this young man's life," he began. "Keep Jerald from the boredom that could lead him away from You."

Pastor Newby's prayers were answered. Over twenty years later, God is still showing me I made the right choice.

And I haven't had time to be bored since.

5

Big Brother, I'm Scared

I put childish ways behind me.
(1 Corinthians 13:11)

OUR NEIGHBORHOOD WAS never the worst in Detroit. (It's still not the worst, but that's nothing to brag about.) We enjoyed the stability of a loving home and good neighbors. Still, there were times when that stability was shaken.

I remember the day when a neighborhood boy—I'll call him Chuck—ran screaming past our house. Chuck was a small, fiery kid who lived in the next block and hung out with a slightly rougher crowd than I was used to. Screaming was out of character for Chuck; he was always trying to make up for being short in stature by being long on toughness.

But this day was different. Chuck seemed much younger and smaller. While Chuck was hanging out with his friends, one of them pulled out a zip gun and "accidentally" shot Chuck in the neck. Chuck didn't wait for an ambulance. He ran through the neighborhood toward his home, holding his neck and crying louder than any tough guy I'd ever seen.

Chuck survived that shooting with only a small scar to show for it. But later in life, the streets caught up with him. The last time I heard about Chuck, he was in prison.

Coming of age was not an easy task for me. In my neighborhood, as in many like it today, children were often forced to grow up before they wanted to. Even though our family tried their hardest to keep the streets outside our house, the streets found a way to penetrate the walls anyway. Our neighborhood was never the worst in town, but we still learned the law of the streets quickly. We had to. We had to know where to go, where not to go, who to trust, and when to keep walking.

We had to grow up.

Violence in the inner city is not new. In fact, fighting is just part of the day-to-day ritual in the lives of many urban young people. I knew some guys who loved to fight—it was their way of communicating. But after seeing them whip a few of my friends, I knew exactly what they were trying to say. I'd hate to see those guys coming, because I knew they were going to try to communicate with me. Being an average fighter most of my life gave me enough of a reputation to avoid most fights, but not all of them. I really don't know how many times my hat was thrown into the ring. However, I'm confident I went through enough scuffles to compile an impressive amateur record. Thankfully, I was never seriously hurt. I can say I only had a few cuts and bruises to show for my trouble. You see, I was a Muhammad Ali fan, and I wanted to get hit as little as possible. My friends and family can tell you one of my mottoes has always been "I'm allergic to pain." I'm happy I don't have any old bullet wounds or healed knife scars to show off!

When I was in my early teens, my father sent my brother John and me to karate lessons. Mr. Shim, a master of Korean karate, taught us along with many other young people from Detroit. Every Saturday morning we would assemble at his studio for a two-hour lesson in the discipline of blocking, kicking, and punching. Master Shim helped to build our confidence as well as our ability.

One of the best things about taking karate in those days was the ability it gave you to bluff your way out of most situations. All you had to do was give a demonstration of your skills.

After taking karate lessons for a couple of years, My brother John, cousin Ulysses Jr., and I became proficient in breaking boards with our hands, our feet, and even our foreheads. One day we decided to show our fathers and grandparents how good we'd become, so we brought some boards home from school to demonstrate. We set up in our living room and gave a quick martial arts demonstration for our families.

When we'd completely dazzled them with our quick hands and powerful feet, we took the remaining boards outside to "finish them off" in our backyard. While we were breaking the rest of the boards, some of the neighborhood boys gathered to watch.

It was amazing how few fights we got into after that. I guess the thought of being split in two like scrap lumber was a great deterrent in those days.

These days, though, karate can do very little for children who are dodging bullets. Except for the discipline it grants, the art of self-defense is pretty senseless in the hood. I know Steven Seagal looks pretty impressive when he disarms two hundred men in an hour-and-a-half movie. His ponytail flaps in the wind as he chops, kicks, slices, and dices the bad guys like a Ginsu knife. But the last time I checked, even the great masters hadn't developed a punch that stops .38 caliber bullets.

After my encounter with the National Guardsman during the riots, the second time a gun was pointed at me I was in the seventh grade. Some friends and I were preparing to enter school when a neighborhood thug eighteen years old or so walked up to us, pulled out a gun, and stuck it in our faces. Because there were seven or eight of us there, he had to swing the gun around in our faces. Back and forth from face to face—we all had the chance to look down the barrel of that gun. He was using a small caliber revolver, probably a .22 caliber "Saturday Night Special." Still, when he pointed it in my face, it looked like a cannon. Just the thought of being shot almost made me wet my pants. My heart was going a hundred miles per second, and I couldn't swallow.

The kicker was that he only wanted our lunch money. We went through all that trauma for a mere forty cents. As big as he was, I would have given him the money *without* the gun! We never told our teachers what happened. We never told anybody. It would have only made things worse.

But things did get worse anyway. Things got *much* worse. In my day there was no such thing as a drive-by shooting. Now children are cut down without even knowing where the shots are coming from. Maybe it's because no one ever said anything.

I remember the old folks saying,"I don't know how these young kids make it nowadays. Things are so bad." I find myself saying the same thing about the children today. How do they make it? Where do they find the courage to go on?

A gun is as common as paper and pencils in many school settings. We hardly flinch when a school shooting is reported on the news. Guns are a fact of life, after all. Young people today are accustomed to violence.

Take my younger brother Andre, for example. Andre spent his entire life in inner city Detroit. For him, violence was just part of the scenery.

My wife, Jerra, and I took the opportunity to visit our friends and relatives in Detroit in 1986. I was excited about seeing my grandparents and the rest of the family. By 1986, Jerra and I had been in Colorado just long enough to feel out of touch with our relatives back east. It felt good to be home in Motown again.

Jerra and I decided to spend a day with Andre. As the youngest of the January family, Andre was the brother with whom I'd spent the least time over the years. Andre and I shared the same father. Although Andre had always lived away from the January house with his mother, Helen, he spent plenty of time around us as he grew older. To all of us, Andre was just another one of the January boys. Everyone knew Andre was high-strung, but they also knew that he was a really great kid. He was no angel, but Helen constantly encouraged him to be the best he could be, and I believe Andre was trying.

Andre was a real talker. Anyone who ever began a conversation with him would be in it for the long haul. Like most teenagers, Andre was preoccupied with his looks and constantly brushed his hair to make sure his waves were looking good. He often talked about girls, and he kept up with the latest fashions, which he wore quite well.

I wish I could recall some of the jokes and funny stories Andre told, but I can clearly remember only our last conversation. The Lord knows I've tried to recall happier times more clearly.

The day of my last conversation with Andre, my wife, Jerra, and I took Andre to the mall. We spent most of our time listening to his crazy jokes and trying to understand his strange taste in clothing. I quickly found out I had a lot of catching up to do with Andre. I especially enjoyed his ideas about the future. We talked about what he wanted to do and where he wanted to go. His goals and dreams seemed boundless.

When we returned to my grandparents' home, Andre pulled me to the side and made a very strange proposal. "Big brother, I'm scared," Andre said. "These people in Detroit are crazy. What if you let me come to live with you and Jerra in Denver during the school year, and I come home in the summers to be with Moms?"

Without blinking, I gave Andre my convenient Christian answer: "I'll pray about it."

We hung around the house for a few more hours. We laughed and had the time of our lives with the family I love.

On the way back to Denver I told Jerra about Andre's request. The conversation evolved into other things, and our discussion about Andre quickly passed. After our return to Denver, it wasn't long before we found ourselves in our normal routine. The days turned into weeks and the weeks into months. I never prayed about Andre's wish to move to Denver. I really wanted to, but I never quite got around to it.

Sounds familiar, doesn't it?

One day in May 1987, I was sitting at my desk at work when I decided to call home to speak with Granddaddy and catch up on the family news.

My brother Jeff answered the phone. After our initial greetings, he stunned me by asking, "Are you coming home for the funeral?"

My mind raced back to two years before. The last time Jeff had answered the phone at my grandparents' house, he had to break the news to me that our half-brother Charles had been shot and killed. Even though I hadn't known Charles well, it was an extreme shock for me. But now—who was it? What had happened?

"Jerald, are you coming home for the funeral?"

I was still in shock from the first time he'd asked. My mind raced as I paused to give him an answer. I didn't even know who had died. The logical answer was that one of my grandparents had passed away. They were getting older. Maybe something had gone wrong with one of them.

Finally I asked, "Who died?"

Jeff was obviously startled by my question. He answered with a question of his own. "Nobody called you?"

Then there was a pause that seemed like an hour. I'm sure that was because of my fear about finding out the answer to my question. Finally, reluctantly, Jeff whispered the news that changed my life forever.

"Andre's dead."

"How did he die?" I asked. It may sound strange, or even wrong on my part, but I was hoping I'd hear that Andre died in some ordinary way. Somehow I felt that would relieve the fear that was growing in my gut. *Please, Jeff, tell me that Andre died of choking or drowning or in a car accident.*

Jeff's answer was the answer I knew was coming. "Andre was shot," he managed to say. "They found him shot several times in the head. They messed him up, man."

I went into shock. I couldn't talk. I didn't want to eat. As I thought of Andre that afternoon as we prepared to travel to Detroit, all I could hear him say was, "Big brother, I'm scared."

Out of all the conversations we had in the past, the only thing that would come to mind was, "Big brother, I'm scared."

"Big brother, I'm scared." Dear Jesus, what had I been thinking?

Andre's wake was on Mother's Day 1987. As we walked into the funeral home, I thought I was going to be strong and show some dignity. But when it was my turn to view Andre's body, I lost it. All my composure went out the window. Andre looked like he was sleeping. His hair was perfectly cut with the waves on top, just as he liked it. My little brother, this handsome young man, sixteen years old, would never see the future he spoke of with such promise. His mother, friends, and family all cried out for Andre in their grief and asked the same question thousands ask every week in this country: "Why?"

No one there had the answer, of course. Very few understand why or how this sort of thing happens, because it doesn't make any sense. I certainly didn't have any answers that day. I sat in my seat saying over and over again, "It's my fault. It's my fault."

Jeff told me later that some people overheard me and assumed I had something to do with Andre's death. They had no way of understanding what I meant.

I had spent all my adult life working with teenagers. In church and as a high school coach of football and basketball, I had prided myself on being an adult that stood up for the rights of young folks. From the design of programs to the initiation of good outreach programs, Jerald January was right there for the young people.

But somehow, I didn't hear my own brother calling out for help. I may have done some good in Jesus' name, but I'd let my little brother down. I'd resorted to the same thing I was quick to accuse others of doing: playing the Christian game. I'd employed clever words and slick slogans to advance my ministerial career before. It was no problem to tell Andre, "I'll pray about it."

"I'll pray about it" sounds Christian. But it was a lie. I never prayed about it, and now I'll never know how God would have led me because I never gave Him a chance to tell me. Because of that I'll never know if Andre would have lived out his dreams. I don't know if the streets would have gotten the better of him, or if Andre would have beaten the streets.

I just don't know. Only God knows.

As I looked at Andre's body for the last time at his funeral, I promised Andre I would never forget him. I promised him I'd tell the world about him. But more important, I promised God that day that if He gave me the time and strength, I would dedicate my life to helping the young people He put in my path. And God has kept me faithful to that promise I made back in 1987. He has allowed me to spend time with some wonderful young people. For many of them, I'm their big brother, and I look at them as my little brothers and sisters. In many ways, they've replaced Andre in my life.

Every time I see young people abusing themselves or someone else, I hear Andre saying, "Big brother, I'm scared." Whenever I see young people who have no hope and end up doing desperate things, I hear Andre saying, "Big brother, I'm scared."

I can't help all of them by myself. No one person can do it all. I know, because I tried to for over a year after Andre's death. But now I pray about every opportunity I have to touch a young person's life.

Our young people have been taught the art of shooting by countless media murders slickly put to music with the latest special effects. They often carry weapons and have no regrets about using them. Many never think of the real damage they are doing to themselves, their families, and the community in which they live. After being shot, one gang member was quoted saying, "I didn't think it would hurt." But the hurt goes deeper and spreads wider than he could ever imagine.

I often talk with young people today who feel they have no

choice but to get involved in potentially fatal battles. In my time the worst that could happen was a black eye or a bloody nose. Your reputation could take a slight thrashing, but no one ever lost his life. Most modern-day bullies, however, are not satisfied with a fist fight. I don't know if any of today's thugs could have survived twenty-five years ago. The ability to compete in a fair fight has been lost over the years.

Violence is in style these days. There is a natural tendency for youngsters to disagree, argue, and even fight on occasion. I doubt that many adults made it through childhood without some kind of altercation. But too many of today's children have bought into the lie that says, "I can never be seen as weak or defenseless, or I'll lose my reputation." They've become convinced that what they see time and again on television and in movies holds the meaning of life. Their surroundings teach them what is important and what is not.

What do children learn from these "teachers"? One lesson is that life is not really important. When children believe that their futures are already determined by society and that they could never be happy with the hand they've been dealt, they feel it's all the more important to alter the future for themselves and anyone who stands in their way. Too many of them have no concept of what God holds for their futures. When children fail to realize that the promises of God far outweigh the lessons of culture, why are we surprised that so many of them become felons—or corpses?

Very few young people I have talked to across this land had a real idea how their actions could lead them to such misery. Somehow, they missed the notion that actions have consequences. But should we be surprised? Children learn by example, and we've been offering them some strange examples to follow. It is obvious to me that if we are ever to stem the flow of today's flood of violence, immorality, and societal suicide, we must first stop the hypocrisy that we display every day.

We punish murderers. We say over and over again that we

should not display violent behavior. Yet we reward visual violence—and it doesn't matter if it depicts drive-by killings or child killers—time and again with high Nielsen ratings and our dollars at the box office. We rail against promiscuity, but then we tune in to soap operas featuring the bed hopper of the week.

Surely this "anything goes for more profit" slant in media has an impact on our children. When they are surrounded by examples of characters who make lousy choices and suffer no real consequences, they're lulled into thinking they can make the same lousy choices and get away with it in real life.

That's tragic, because the stakes are so much higher for young people today. During my youth, we made tons of mistakes. The difference is that our mistakes were the kind that usually allowed us the opportunity to live and try again. That's not the case for thousands of teenagers in our country. The mistakes of today's youth are too often "forever mistakes"—things that change their lives with one hit. Unplanned pregnancies, experimentation with drugs, violent crimes, and drive-by shootings all begin with lousy choices and end in scarred lives.

If I see my son about to eat something I know is poisonous, but for any reason refuse to stop him, then it's my fault when he dies. The same can be said for any of us who simply stand by and watch the future generation fill their heads and hearts with things that may lead to their destruction. I'll never be one to say we need a ban on what people say and how they say it. But I am saying that, as a society, we've taken our constitutional rights to free expression to an all-time low. One corrective action we must take is to raise our voices in our own homes and help our children discern what is good and what is not.

We have an obligation to reward and recognize those in our society who are examples of real excellence. We also have an obligation to our children to recognize those who are making themselves wealthy by pushing the mindless mush and raunch that disconnect actions and consequences.

By the time I was ready to leave high school I had seen plenty. My journey into reality had been launched. The fairy tales of my past had been replaced with the technicolor reality of inner-city Detroit: the good, the bad, and the ugly. My life hardly resembled that of the weekly television sitcom youth. The air-waves were filled with the joyful sounds of cotton candy teenagers from *The Partridge Family* and *The Brady Bunch*. Every week the saga continued of the challenges that gripped the lives of America's favorite families. Would Marcia get her braces off in time for the prom? Would Bobby raise enough money to get Mom Brady a special present? Could Danny pass his math test?

Boy, what problems to have. I often thought I could thrive in that neighborhood. (Where did they live anyway? Come to think of it, there weren't many guys like me coming over for cookies and milk, were there? Would the Bradys have moved away if the Januarys moved in next door?)

Like most teenagers, I learned soon after starting high school that I could probably get away with anything I wanted. *I'm almost grown and they can't see me anyway*, I thought. *If I don't go to class, how will they know? If I smoke cigarettes, that's my business.* The fact was simple: I could do whatever I wanted. I could hang out with whomever I wanted. Good or bad, it didn't matter. What they taught me at school or at home didn't matter anymore. What I decided now was what mattered. Should I get a gun? Should I have sex? Should I smoke weed?

All these decisions. Decisions, decisions. Maybe I was too young to make those kinds of decisions. But age was no excuse then, or today. The fact of the matter is *all* our kids have to make hard decisions, especially in their teenage years. Unfortunately, many young people are making the kind of choices that lead them to a dead end, or at least to a very bumpy road.

Thankfully, I was raised by a family that believed Proverbs 22:6: "Train a child in the way he should go, and when he is old he will not turn from it." Everybody has to make choices. All of them are not easy. Nevertheless, they must be made.

One more thing. Our government says it is looking for ways to "stop the killing," while at the same time we pay billions to kill unborn babies. This kind of logic is crazy. We legislate laws to save our most precious resource, our children. Then at the same time we pass laws so we can kill all those unborn souls before they get a chance to make their mark.

Who are we kidding? The reality is we can't have it both ways. Life or death, you choose. Andre's death at sixteen weeks in the womb would have been just as tragic as it was sixteen years into his walk on earth.

Seems to me that innocent blood is innocent blood no matter who spills it.

Part 3
College and Career

Teammates at Ferris State

As host of the New Visions television show, I sometimes took the show "out on the road."

I love working with the children God has placed in my life.

6 Those Good Old College Days

Be transformed by the renewing of your mind.
(Romans 12:2)

DO YOU REMEMBER the commercials for the United Negro College Fund that say "A mind is a terrible thing to waste?" For years UNCF has helped young African American students get through traditionally black colleges. Unfortunately, while I was in high school there were no UNCF representatives frequenting the halls of Central High. Or if they were there, I never saw them.

Maybe I should have gone looking for them. *But why should I?* I thought. Everybody on our football team—even the second stringers—was getting offers to play ball in college. Surely I would find my name on some scholarship list. And as a new Christian, my confidence level was high. I figured God would provide.

The truth is I was just an average student most years of high school. As is often the case, that was my choice. I did enough to get by, except for art classes. Art was my passion. For most students art was just an elective in which you could score a C just by showing up. For me art offered the chance to shine and gain an identity of my own.

I loved football and the excitement of the games. Like most high school ball players I had the dreams of the NFL and the good life that went with it. But I was too slow to be a running back and too small to be a threat on the line. Besides, I played behind an All-State linebacker. At most schools I'm sure I would have started or played a significant position somewhere, but not at Central.

I tried out for the tennis team too and made it, mostly because tennis was not one of the most popular sports in the hood. As a matter of fact, tennis, swimming, and golf were the only teams just about anybody could make. You could probably join the swim team at Central even if you couldn't swim. Anyway, in tennis I played second doubles with a guy who was worse than me. What's even crazier—we actually won a couple of matches.

I remember going into the city tournament in the spring of 1974. (Everybody got to go to the city tournament, no matter how sorry you were.) I was pretty psyched up for it. My grandmother bought me a new tennis shirt just for the occasion. It was white with blue trim, our school colors. As we arrived at the tournament, I was excited to see the crowd that had assembled. There were television news crews, newspaper reporters, and plenty of cute girls. I remember thinking, "I could get used to this action. Yeah, buddy! Women, press, and no big funky guys beating my brains out."

I headed for the match board to see who our first opponents would be. I was hoping to face a couple of those sorry guys we had already beaten. If we could win our first match, I was sure I could talk to one of the young ladies hanging around the courts. Maybe we'd even have time for a Coke and a smile or something. But when I saw the names on the match board, I stopped dead in my tracks. We were scheduled to play Mumford High School, which had the best tennis team in the city, and probably in the state as well. These brothers believed in tennis like I believed in God. They even had matching tennis shoes.

Need I tell you that the brothers from Mumford beat us like we stole something? I would have rather played football against Dick Butkus and the Chicago Bears than go through that kind of humiliation. Tennis balls were flying by faster than a speeding bullet. The pretty girls were bent over laughing so hard that all I remember about them were the tops of their heads.

I never played tennis again. Never.

That's why I loved art so much. I was actually pretty good at it, and I even made spare money doing portraits for a while. I drew with pencil or charcoal, and each drawing took hours to complete. I actually got more satisfaction out of the reaction of the people I worked for than the money. My art teacher, Mr. Nanstanski, had plenty of patience with all his students. But he taught those with talent the special things about art that actually made it fun. He even got some of my work displayed in The Board of Education building. I had made up my mind that should I ever get to college I would major in some type of art-related field.

Sometime during my second year of school I was informed that the amount of credits earned determined when you could graduate. I had taken tons of credits and was ahead of schedule. By the time I was seventeen years old I was tired of Central. Yes, there were some good times there. There just weren't enough good times to keep me at Central another year. Coach Woody, an assistant football and head track coach, told me that if I ran track and stayed for my last year of eligibility he could get me a scholarship to Jackson State University in Jackson, Mississippi. He told me I would probably grow and increase my speed during that extra year. As tempting as the offer sounded, I decided to declare myself a senior and get out while the getting was good.

All the while my mind was still on getting into college somehow. There were no offers for football scholarships, not even from Division Two schools. Finally, I decided that maybe I could walk on somewhere if I could get enough money together to pay for first semester classes. My father and grandparents were encouraging me to attend Wayne State University in Detroit. I told them I'd rather work in the factory than attend Wayne State. Not that Wayne wasn't and isn't a fine school; I just wanted to go to college somewhere besides Detroit. We debated back and forth about where I should attend college, while time to make that decision was running out.

One day while walking down the hallway at Central I was approached by my guidance counselor. Her name was Eunice High. Mrs. High was the younger sister of Joe Louis, the famous boxer. That's right: Joe Louis's sister was my counselor in high school. You never knew if people were lying to you, but I had seen her in *Jet Magazine* with her brother a couple of times. She definitely was the real deal.

I'd never spoken to Mrs. High much before then. She said, "Jerald, are you thinking of going to college?"

"Yes," I replied.

"Well, there's a college that needs more black students. It's outside of Detroit. Why don't you come and talk to me about it at my office?"

I agreed, and later that day we met in Mrs. High's office. She informed me that the school was Ferris State College in Big Rapids, Michigan.

"You mean Grand Rapids," I replied.

"No, *Big* Rapids."

I applied to Ferris, took all the appropriate tests that high school seniors were required to take for admission to college, and was accepted as a freshman at Ferris State College.

I was seventeen years old when I graduated from Central in the early summer of 1974. For years since, I've wondered if I would have been better off staying one more year in high school. Coach Woody turned out to be right. I grew some during the summer, and surely would have done better as a high school player rather than a college player that fall.

But college was a different ballgame anyway. More than that, it proved to be a whole new world. A month or so before school started I was on my way to Big Rapids for freshman orientation. Incoming freshmen during orientation were known as "the three day wonders." Three days of tours, speeches, win-ing, and dining—all at the expense of the school. On the bus trip up I met several other Detroit inner-city kids who were on their way as well. Some of them had never been outside of Detroit. I had the advantage of having been a frequent traveler to Toledo, Ohio, and Evergreen, Alabama. My new acquaintances made the 100-plus-mile ride enjoyable as we compared old high school stories.

I'll never forget my first impressions of Big Rapids. *This has to be the original Mayberry*, I thought. The town had beautiful tree-lined streets, cute little shops, and one movie theater. Just one. The campus was bigger than I imagined, and that was a relief. I had been hoping for more than three buildings on campus.

As we toured the campus, I realized why the college was looking for more black students. They didn't have very many. For the first time in my life I realized what the word *minority* meant. We were clearly the minority (read "less or fewer than") group on campus. Central High School was the only 100 percent black high school in the state of Michigan when I attended. Being a minority at Central meant you were left-handed. But Ferris was a different story altogether.

I became a member of a whole new society, a society that I had only been privy to through television and a couple of high school football games. The white world was a new frontier. All I really knew before Ferris State was that white kids laid in the sun a lot and clapped on the wrong beat. Now I was going to get the chance to see these people up close and personal.

I always got the impression that white students were much smarter. At least on television, they were always smarter. My grandparents told me I always had to be twice as smart to get half as far as a white kid. That thought stayed with me as I prepared for my first quarter of college.

My father drove me to school that first fall at Ferris. My head was spinning as we sped past one farm, then another, then another. Going to college had been my choice, and I couldn't show any fear or resignation.

My father helped me unload all my junk in my dormitory. Pennock Hall, room 409, top bunk was my new address. He shook my hand, looked me in the eye, and said, "You wanted to be here. Don't come home until you graduate." We laughed and said our good-byes.

Deep inside I knew my father was very proud of me for attending college. As he drove away I felt an emotion that was new to me: loneliness. My only friend now was Jesus, and I didn't know Him all that well.

Surprisingly, I found that some things at Ferris were easier than home. The football practices were a piece of cake compared to those I endured on the rock and dirt fields in Detroit. Some of the freshman courses I was required to take were very easy. The lunchroom food was much better than Central's; I could actually recognize most of the meats that were served. The Big Rapids theater had a new movie every Monday, which was "Students' Night." As the weeks and months passed, the loneliness I felt when I thought of my loved ones at home eased.

There were other things, however, that were much more difficult to get used to. The fact alone that "Hee-Haw" came on television almost every day was enough to make me want to drop out of school. There were the cross-campus walks to class in the bitter cold. (I soon learned to cut through every building on campus—including the girls' dorms.) And for a long time I lacked the kind of social life I'd enjoyed in Detroit.

One evening, for example, my roommate and I went to McDonald's for dinner. When we saw there were no empty tables, we asked two sisters if we could eat with them. Without hesitating they said, "We're upper classmen, not freshmen."

For heaven's sake, we just wanted to sit down and eat our Big Macs, not get married! It's a shame when you spend all those grade school years establishing your reputation and then get to college and learn you're a minus again.

Let me state for the record that I appreciate my alma mater more than words can say. Some of the things I encountered on the Ferris State campus in those days probably would have happened on most, if not all, of the predominantly white campuses across the country. Many African American students today find themselves in the same situations I found myself in back in the seventies. But I believe now, as then, that even situations completely foreign to them can be the keys to their future success if they can find the wisdom and dignity to deal with those very challenges.

I suppose the biggest challenges of my college days came under one of the three C's: Class, Color, or Culture. I had to learn to understand them and live with them on a daily basis.

Class is defined as "a social stratum whose members share similar characteristics." The terms *lower class, middle class*, and *upper class* were words seldom or never mentioned around my house. We lived in a community where the class of people didn't appear to matter much. While I was growing up I really enjoyed the Temptations' song "Don't Let the Jones Get You Down." The song spoke about how futile it is for those of us of normal means to try to live like those of extraordinary means. But in college I found that the class with which you were identified could mean the difference in how you were treated and whose company you kept. Class didn't come into play much with me because of my race. But I observed that many of the white students played hard at the class game. I saw students who would do almost anything to be accepted by the yuppie, preppy crowd. The smugness and superior attitude that was manifested by "the elites"—pronounced "e-lights"—were worn like a good suit.

Over the years I've noticed how the class system is still used to make one group of people feel or seem somehow superior to others. Take flying, for example. I travel quite a bit because of my speaking and meeting schedule, and it never ceases to amaze me how the passengers in first class are treated as compared to the rest of the passengers. All the special things they receive in first class—like leg room and digestible food—are enough to give the rest of us inferiority complexes. What's even more hilarious is the way some of those first-class folks look at you when you're on your way to the rear of the plane, an area I affectionately call "The Aviation Ghetto." It must be hard for many passengers who long to sit in the front of the plane to be forced to sit in the back. It must be an even stranger feeling not to be able to use the bathroom in first class. The way many of the passengers push and shove to be the first off the plane makes it seem like it's humiliating to sit over the wing.

I've learned the class system is a part of life in this country. While it is somehow a necessary part of our society, it is just another form of separation that keeps people from really knowing each other.

Culture is defined as "the totality of socially transmitted behavior patterns characteristic of a people." Every group of people in this country has a culture. They have unique ways of relating to each other and certain things that they value. Culture is the distinctive signature of a people, setting them apart from the rest of the world.

My first trip into the real world taught me that my culture wasn't always deemed important by the outside world. Everything from the clothes I wore to the music I listened to became the brunt of jokes or ridicule. The things in my culture that seemed normal to me and that gave me identity were now funny, or worse, unimportant. The joke was somehow on me.

From Oktoberfest to St. Patrick's Day, the cultural experience of the majority culture on campus was displayed with pride and enthusiasm. One tradition after another was paraded across the school grounds like proud ducks in a row. I learned plenty about the traditions of my schoolmates that enriched my life, or at least cleared up some questions. I even joined some of my pals in their celebrations. These events were considered the "normal" things to do, after all. But they were not normal to me or to the other black students on campus. If we didn't participate, though, we could be labeled "ignorant." I guess we could have been called worse, but who really were the ignorant ones?

While we were oblivious to some of the holidays, customs, and celebrations of our white schoolmates, they were almost completely ignorant to the ways of black folks. I had never seen any kids who were as naïve to the culture of others as the people I came across on campus.

One weekend, totally by chance, I found myself in the dorm surrounded by white students talking about their hometowns. They informed me about life in the suburbs or on the farm. Most of it was old news, but they were friendly and like anyone else they wanted to talk about the things that made them feel special. Finally, someone asked about my home in Detroit. I gave a brief overview of my family and thought that would be it. One guy named Paul, who grew up on the farm, started asking me question. Genuinely curious, he asked questions like "Do all black men really carry knives? Do black folk really drink a lot of chocolate milk to keep their skin dark and smooth?" And the list went on and on. The conversation quickly progressed to serious cultural questions, and we sat for a couple of hours talking about life in my world.

This exchange soon became a monthly event. I termed the time "Colored Life Stories." Maybe these guys didn't have much of a social life, but it didn't matter to me. They wanted to know about my people, culture, and community and I had no problem telling them. Even today, I tell my white friends and associates that if they really want to know about my culture I'll stay up all night to discuss it with them. The problem is that too many with whom I come in contact still consider my culture—and many others—unimportant or laughable.

Last but certainly not least is the *C* of Color. Race by far is the most controversial of the three C's. To me, it is the strangest as well, because it is the hardest for people to deal with.

Growing up my favorite color was and still is dark blue. It speaks of royalty and coolness. Dark blue has always set right with me. I never really cared much for white. It was one of those colors that just sat there. But when you combine white with blue, the results are amazing. As I mentioned earlier, the Central High School colors were blue and white. That combination of colors is still one of my favorites today.

In our society we don't care much about mixing colors. But mixing *people* of different colors is one of the things that gets us worked up the most. Yeah, I know songs like "We Are the World" make us feel kind of cuddly. But the song only lasts about four minutes. What do we do when the music stops playing? For many, when the music stops, the "cuddly" goes away. Real life is quite different than the make-believe world we retreat to in our imaginations, or even in music.

The easiest way to categorize our hate is by picking our favorite color and devaluing the rest. I mentioned earlier that I had made up my mind should I ever get to college I would major in some art-related field. At Ferris State, I majored in commercial art. During the first quarter of classes several other black students and I found ourselves assembled in the office of one of our instructors, an old crusty guy who was known to be way past his prime. Somehow he got on the subject of different "types of students." And then he made a statement that I will never forget: "For some reason you people just don't have what it takes to make it in this field. I would suggest you transfer to something else."

His remark made me mad. I knew that all he wanted to do was scare us off. And he did: almost every black student that heard his comment dropped commercial art as a major—except me. I stayed just to prove him wrong.

At times I really felt I should transfer. I didn't always like the curriculum or the work as much as I thought I would. But for better or worse, this professor's remark was the catapult that hurled me toward my degree. The bigger issue is not how many students this instructor discouraged over the years, but why he discouraged them. I vowed to make him look at me walk across the stage at graduation time, and I did. I'm very proud of my degree. Even now the certificate sits prominently displayed in my home office.

Another Color issue arose in the area of campus ministries. My pastor had counseled me to find a Bible study or worship group to join when I got to school. So trying to be an obedient young believer, I set out to find other Christians. I attended a few Bible studies and social functions, but my times there were always a bit tense. At first I thought the tension came solely from me. I was still quite shy in those days and felt I needed to talk to others if I expected them to talk to me. Surely, I thought, after a couple of visits the other kids would warm up to me. But they never did. I would try to be friendly, and the best I got was a phony smile. The only thing I could attribute their coolness to was my race. White Christian students on campus were no more accustomed to worshiping with black students than their parents were.

I finally became acquainted with other black Christians on campus. Many of their stories were similar to mine. Finally, we created our own Christian organization called "Youth Ambassadors for Christ." While we had our own church services and Bible studies, we did fellowship with the other groups. Our functions seemed to be less tense that way. Having our own group seemed to take the pressure off the other campus ministries to include us in their plans.

During one of our joint Christian meetings a young white student rose to tell our combined groups, "While we should love one another and be friends, we should be careful not to get too close. I'm afraid this could be the start of the One World Church the Bible speaks about."

Talk about insulting. Now I was being compared to the Beast or the False Prophet!

When graduation approached I began to enjoy a deep feeling of accomplishment. I asked my brother John to bring my grandmother to Ferris State for the ceremony. It was Mama's first and only trip to the campus, and she was very excited to be there. My best friend Donald Williams came with his wife, Barbara, to join us for the occasion. We took the opportunity to tour the campus and meet some of my friends. After a while, my grandmother spread a blanket out on the lawn in front of my dorm and sat beneath a newly blossomed tree. Her smile and sense of contentment made all the days of cold weather and cold attitudes worth the struggle.

The graduation ceremony was held in the football stadium. I looked for the teacher who told me I would never make it. I wanted him to see that I *did* make it and that he'd been wrong about me and my people. I also looked for Mama. I wanted her to see me, but I didn't think I would spot her in the sea of faces on the stands.

Then I heard her voice. "There he is!" she shouted.

Later, Mama told me that it was easy to pick me out of the crowd. "You looked like a fly in a bowl of buttermilk," she said.

Much of what I learned in college was never listed in the school catalog. And things in the past twenty years have changed. Ferris State College is now Ferris State University. The campus is much larger than when I attended. The school even has a minority affairs department and an African American affairs department. I know plenty of schools who can't come close to that kind of progress.

Unfortunately, progress on the institutional front doesn't always mean progress on the personal front. Institutions only provide structures for interaction. We make or break the quality of relationships across class, cultural, or color lines. What we assume about each other is usually far more damaging than what we ask about each other.

That's why I'll gladly relate more to a young man from the farm who is trying to find out more about me than to an educated fool who has already determined my worth based on his biases. College should be a time to expand your horizons, and we all need others who aren't like us to make that happen.

If we remain trapped in the patterns of the past, we're wasting opportunities. Color, class, and culture don't make anyone inherently superior. But the chance to learn from others to understand them more could make us better people. If we do not take those opportunities to learn and grow, we may well be remembered in history as "The Generation of Wasted Minds."

7 The Call

The LORD your God will be with you
wherever you go.
(Joshua 1:9)

AS THAT FINAL year at Ferris came to a close, I knew where I was going. I was engaged to be married to a young lady I met a year earlier on campus. I had a job lined up in Chicago with a growing company. Things were looking up. I had a sense of expectancy that everything would be smooth sailing.

Graduation could not have come at a better time. I loved all the relationships that had developed from my time at Ferris, but I was ready to move on. My mind was set on bigger fish. There had to be more that the Lord wanted for my life, and I was going to find it.

I had already learned that God sometimes had a mind of his own as to what he wanted me to do with my life, for He had already radically altered my plans during my sophomore year when He called me into the ministry. At that time I had no intention, dream, vision, or desire to preach. If God had all the resources of the universe available to Him, He surely didn't need me. But yet He called me to enter the ministry.

It's not easy to explain what "the call" feels like. In fact, before my call, I had heard of God's calling from others and felt sorry for the poor folks who had to endure such a burden. I knew it had to be an overwhelming task to stand before a congregation and preach. To me, preaching was a crazy way of getting a message across, anyway. You're yelling your lungs out to those who, in many cases, are simply hoping you'll hurry up and sit down. Many times you're the only thing standing between them and a good fried chicken dinner. Who needed that kind of aggravation anyway? Being an amateur comedian at the Apollo in Harlem is easier than preaching in many of the churches in this country. For a shy person like me, having to preach would be the biggest nightmare in God's universe.

I never desired to be in front of people in any manner. I looked up to men like my pastor, who could hold the attention of an audience as if he were offering them pure gold. People like him had a gift that could only be heaven sent. The rest of us were put here for other reasons. My mind was made up to serve God in a way that would honor Him behind the scenes, probably through my talents in art or as a deacon in church.

There are those who enter the pulpit ministry for attention, fame, or money. History has documented countless numbers of pretenders to the cloth. Every kind of person from hustlers to Casanovas have imitated the called of God in our land. There's an old rhyme about preachers that says, "Some were called and some were sent. Others just got up one day and went." One thing my grandmother constantly said was "Boy, don't ever play with God."

So when the call came, I could not ignore it.

One evening in the spring of my sophomore year, some of us decided to gather in one of the dorms to pray for God's direction for the upcoming summer. We read some Scripture and sang a hymn. We then selected separate portions of the room and prayed alone. I crouched down in a corner and began to pray. "God, what do You want me to do?" I prayed. "Please reveal Your will, Lord, for my summer."

Suddenly, as if someone turned on a television set before me, I saw a place filled with fire and dark smoke. I heard loud screaming and yelling and could not tell where it was coming from. It seemed like I was dreaming, except I was wide awake. I was terrified. I opened my eyes, but the nightmare continued.

The vision lasted only a few minutes, but I knew that this was God's way of telling me I had to preach, not for my sake, but for those who would hear what I would say about God and respond.

That night I could not sleep at all. I sat up in a chair in my room and waited for the sun to rise. The screams stayed in my head all night, and for the first time I understood the seriousness of eternal damnation.

After accepting that God had indeed chosen me to be a minister of the Gospel, I called my pastor. It was just 8:00 A.M., but Reverend Newby seemed to be awaiting my call. In fact, after the initial hello he simply said, "So you're ready to preach."

Startled, I replied, "Yes."

In the tradition of the black Missionary Baptist church, Pastor Newby set up a trial sermon date for me. A trial sermon is like an audition for a part in a movie or a play. Your trial sermon often comes before any Bible college or seminary training. The church believes that if you are truly called, there will be a spark in your first sermon.

When my time arrived I was scared to death. Looking out on the audience, all I saw was an endless sea of brown eyes all staring at me like I was an alien who had just landed in the hood. There seemed to be thousands of people there that day, although it was probably more like one hundred fifty.

My hands, knees, and assorted body parts shook uncontrollably as I stood on the main floor of the New Mt. Zion Missionary Baptist Church. I dreamed of being cool, calm, and in control. I wanted to dazzle the audience with an oratorical exhibition not enjoyed since Dr. Martin Luther King's speech on the steps of the Washington Monument. But what they got was the nervous, sweating, often rambling first sermon of a young man who was bent on pleasing God. The title of that message was "I'm Ready." Whether or not I was ready was clearly up for debate. But with all the sweat, nerves, and stammering came a peace within my soul that said, "You're doing the right thing."

When my sermon was over I had to be helped from the sanctuary. I had never felt that kind of tiredness before. It wasn't like the kind of fatigue you experience after a ball game. This came from within, like someone had reached down inside me and pulled out a part of my soul. But it felt good.

The church voted and decided there was indeed some cause to believe I had been called to the ministry. Two weeks later Pastor Newby issued a ministerial license to me to pursue my call. He invited me to sit in the pulpit with all the old guys. I was now part of a unique fraternity. His advice to me still rings in my ear: "Don't step down from this office to be the President of the United States." From that evening on I would be known as Minister January.

Following the advice of my family and pastor I returned that fall to Ferris to complete my commercial art degree. The Youth Ambassadors voted for officers, and I was elected vice president. While I was completely surprised and pleased, the duties added to my already full schedule. I was working part time, coaching student football, studying, and now preaching as well. Often I was asked to preach at our Youth Ambassadors worship services.

If you think preaching to a regular church is hard, try speaking in front of college students. Most of them were smarter than me anyway, and that made things even harder. My first two attempts at preaching on campus were disasters. The truth is I was just plain boring. During the altar prayer of my first campus sermon I was so bad I almost fell asleep as I leaned on the podium. Again the doubt began to creep into my mind. *Maybe I'm supposed to preach only to old people. At least they clapped for me during the trial sermon*, I thought. Ronnie, our president, and some of the others seemed comfortable and at home speaking to a collegiate crowd. But I sure didn't.

The turning point came when I was asked to speak again. This time I decided to fast for three days prior to the service, and if I failed just as miserably this time, I wouldn't preach again. Keep in mind, fasting was not a regular practice in my circles. As a matter of fact, I'd never really heard much about it until I was in college. But that Thursday, Friday, and Saturday I ate nothing, only pausing at the end of the day to drink a glass of water.

Going to school and working on an empty stomach is not what I would normally recommend as a wise course of action. But as I stood before the students that Sunday morning, I was sure once again that this was where I belonged. The words came more easily, the altar call was heeded, and for the first time souls under my ministry came to Christ.

In the spring of 1977, the Youth Ambassadors traveled to Michigan State University in East Lansing to hear an evangelist speak. At the close of his message the evangelist called for those who wanted special prayer to line up. One by one he prayed for folks who desired to hear a word from the Lord. At times he would speak to individuals specifically as he heard from God.

Over the years I've seen and heard many Christians who could guess a person's lifestyle or past. Some of these people were so vague in their guesses that what they said could be true of anyone. But this gentleman was very accurate when he spoke to my friends. Since he had no idea we would be there, I was convinced he was genuine. However, I really didn't want to hear a word from him or anybody else. Things were going good for me. I knew what my life held for the most part. I didn't need a word from God. Besides, the line was too long. I didn't want to stand for any extended period of time. So as the others continued to stand and wait their turn, I was content to relax in my seat.

As the moments crept by and God's Spirit seemed to fill the room, I began to feel that possibly I could use the prayer. After all, I was about to start a new chapter in my life in a new city. Perhaps God wanted to convey something to me. At the very least the prayer would be welcome.

But again I felt the line was much too long. As is often the case when God is truly using someone, the line got longer. People had waited to see what was happening before they made up their minds to respond to the altar call. My late response would only reflect the same "wait and see" attitude. So I thought, *Forget it. If God wants to say something to me through this guy, He's going to have to call me out of the audience and speak to me.*

At that very second the evangelist, who was praying with a young lady, stopped and turned toward the audience. He looked out in the crowd and pointed and said, "You! Come here." Those of us in our seats were startled, as were the others in line. People began to turn around and look at each other and ask, "Who, me?" I was looking around also, trying to pick out the person that was causing this disruption.

The evangelist pointed again and said, "You, come here." He was pointing at *me*!

I guess God wants to talk to me, I thought.

As I walked toward the evangelist, every eye in the place was on me. But all I could focus on was the awesome realization that God had heard my thoughts. Once again I was amazed at His love, concern, and awareness of my insignificant life.

As I stepped onto the platform, the evangelist—whose name I cannot recall—ordered me to take off my shoes, for the ground I was walking on was holy ground. I complied quickly. Then he asked someone standing nearby to hand him a Bible. Quickly he turned to a passage of Scripture I did not recall having heard in my four years as a Christian: Joshua 1:9. "Have I not commanded you? Be strong and courageous. Do not be terrified; do not be discouraged, for the LORD your God will be with you wherever you go."

I stood in silence, stunned. What could this mean?

I immediately received my answer. This precious brother, who had never seen me before and to my knowledge has never seen me since, spoke to me as if he'd known me all my life. He told me specific things about my future. He told me that if I knew all about my future and the difficulties it would hold, that I'd never want to enter the ministry. He talked with me about my past. He brought up my struggles with loneliness and my desire to fit in somewhere. He told me about my days of playing second-string—not just in athletics, but in many other areas where I stayed behind the scenes in a supporting role. He said that God would allow me to accomplish more for Him than I had ever imagined. And he said that although I was one of the least talented and revered among my peers, God would someday use me to speak to thousands. Then he reminded me again, "Always remember to be strong and courageous."

As I walked back to my seat with my shoes in my hand, I had no idea of all the things that awaited me in Chicago. I knew, however, that Joshua 1:9 would go with me wherever I went.

Most of us never accomplish what God has for us—not because we don't have the opportunity, not because God has forgotten His promises, not because God doesn't know what we need. It's all because we are scared. We so quickly forget that our success is not dependent on us, but on the Spirit of God working through us.

"Do not be terrified; do not be discouraged." We all have disappointments that make us feel there are no reasons to go on. But God is saying to us, "Don't be disheartened, for the Lord your God will be with you wherever you go."

Go means to move, to proceed, to depart, to be about to do, to circulate, to tend, to be guided, to be alienated, to reach, to avail, to become, and even to die. *Go* is obviously an action word. God fully intends us to be action people. Some people may have to take more action than others, but we've got to go nevertheless.

Throughout Scripture God's direction concerning our actions is sure. Proverbs 20:24 says, "Man's goings are of the LORD" (KJV). The writer of Psalm 71:16 sounds confident as he says, "I will go in the strength of the Lord" (KJV). Psalm 17:5 commits a believer's steps to God: "Hold up my goings in thy paths, that my footsteps slip not" (KJV). Psalms 40:2 describes some of the results of salvation: "He brought me up also out of an horrible pit, out of the miry clay, and set my feet upon a rock, and established my goings" (KJV). The heart of the Great Commission of Matthew 28:19 is this: "Go ye therefore and teach all nations" (KJV).

After that service at Michigan State I thought I knew where my life was going. My life was so picture perfect. After moving to Chicago shortly after graduation, however, everything didn't quite work out as I planned. The job didn't last, and neither did the marriage.

But God was there, and He saw me through it all.

Waiting for Heroes That Never Show Up

Then I heard the voice of the Lord saying,
"Whom shall I send ? And who will go for us?"
And I said, "Here am I. Send me!"
(Isaiah 6:8)

I ARRIVED IN Chicago with all the wonder and amazement of a schoolboy on his first day in class.

It was the summer of 1977, barely one month after my graduation from college. I packed up my old mint green Chevrolet Impala that was a graduation gift from my grandfather and headed to Chi-Town.

Though I had lived in the city of Detroit most of my life, Chicago was a new and exciting experience. I thought Detroit was crowded until I saw the masses in Chicago. Downtown Chicago was an experience in itself. It reminded me of the crowds that had frequented downtown Detroit in the early days—except that the people in Chicago must have invited all their friends to come with them! Chicago was one lively city, with the big stores, great restaurants, and plenty of street vendors to prove it.

The sports scene was different than Detroit's, of course. I grew up cheering for the Lions, Tigers, and Pistons. (The Red Wings, Detroit's professional hockey team, wasn't big in my community. There were no black guys on the team, and there were no ice rinks in the hood.) In Chicago I suddenly found myself in the den of my former enemies: the Bulls, Bears, and White Sox. (The Cubs didn't count. I always felt sorry for them.)

I eventually learned it was safer to be a Chicago sports fan than to be loyal to the Detroit teams.

I discovered other differences as I became more familiar with "the Windy City." Take music, for example. Detroit had the Motown Sound, while Chicago was famous for the Blues. The weather provided contrast, too. Detroit is known for the long gray winters. But Chicago is known worldwide for "The Hawk," that howling, piercing wind that blows from Lake Michigan. My first winter in Chicago I actually cried one day because I was so cold.

The Motor City was famous for cars, and Chicago had the famous commuter system. I had never seen a commuter train until I arrived in Chicago. The El train is a trip everybody needs to take at least once. It's loud, crowded, cold in the winter, and hot in the summer. But if you want to avoid the ungodly traffic jams during the daily rush hours, it's the only way to travel.

Another distinct difference between the two cities was the churches. On the surface, church is church. But there is a difference that I caught on to in the first year there, and that difference centered mostly in the music. While the black gospel music scene was awesome in Detroit, it could not compare to the tradition in Chicago. Many of the artists that I played on my radio show at Ferris State were alive, well, and singing every Sunday morning in Chicago. Everyone from the late Mahalia Jackson to the top choirs in the country was from Chicago. And let there be no doubt about it, this was real *Gospel* music. The other music was just religious singing.

While I thank God for all my brothers and sisters from other cultures who lift up God in their own way through music, in my opinion black-style Gospel music is the best by far. The sounds and rhythm along with the heartfelt voices singing deep-rooted lyrics can lift heavy emotional and spiritual burdens. Traditional, contemporary, jazz, or rap, it all sounds great to me. When the religious music awards give only a passing, almost insulting, glance at the talent of these tremendously talented individuals and groups, it is indeed their loss.

Many Christian radio stations refuse to play the songs of most contemporary black and urban artists and then wonder why their market share is so low. Strangely enough, their contemporaries on the secular side have come to the conclusion that African American and urban music not only sells but also increases the ratings. It really seems to me that religious stations are still stuck in a 1950s mind-set of music programming. Many station managers and owners hold on to a long-standing opinion that their listeners won't understand the presentation or style of the Gospel music that springs from the city. Maybe they're afraid their audience might like it too much! The truth is, by playing Gospel music they will probably gain many additional listeners who have tuned out their station because it doesn't compete with those on the secular side. When I did radio in Big Rapids, Chicago, and Denver I always had plenty of listeners—black, white, and others—who called and asked, "Where can I get that record?" or "Who was that?" As the old commercial said, "Try it. You'll like it." And so will your listeners.

As I became more familiar with Chicago, I recognized a large gulf between the races. Chicago is traditionally broken into racially and culturally diverse communities. The Poles, Italians, Hispanics, Asians, and African Americans—to name just a few—have their own predominant pockets of the city. People who dare defy those boundaries often find themselves in the kind of difficult situation that is akin to stepping onto a rival gang's turf. The message is quite clear: "Stay with your own kind." I had to learn that lesson the hard way.

On more than one occasion I was reminded that I was the wrong color for certain facets of the American dream. For example, my wife and I once tried to rent a nicer apartment in an upscale suburb of Chicago. We had been married about a year, and we were both working. Our first home was a small apartment on the south side of Chicago. While it had served its purpose well, we thought that it was time to move up a little.

We saw an ad in the paper that described what we thought would be the perfect place for us. It was in one of the western suburbs that was a "better" neighborhood. It also had better access to transportation and shopping. I called and spoke to the management office, and they were quite friendly. I gave them most of the information they requested over the phone and was told I qualified easily for the apartment I wanted. We made an appointment for later that day to see our new two-bedroom apartment. All the way to the apartment we talked about how nice it would be to move into a new place. Yes, this was indeed why I went to college and worked so hard on my job. This was truly the America I learned about in history class, the place of life, liberty, and the pursuit of happiness.

As we pulled into the parking lot, I was taken by the neat lawn and shrubs that surrounded the complex. Just then I noticed a woman running out of the door. I parked and stepped from the car. *How odd*, I thought. *Why is someone coming to the car to meet us?*

The young white lady was indeed the person I had spoken to on the phone earlier that day. However, once she got a look at my complexion, she was not interested in my qualifications. Her first words to me were, "No, no, no." Before I could get my entire name out of my mouth to introduce myself she continued, "We don't rent to colored people here. There is an apartment complex three miles that way that rents to colored people. I didn't know you were colored on the phone. I'm sorry you drove out here, but you can't live here."

With that, she turned and walked away.

She didn't want to see my college degree. The money in my checking account didn't matter at all. I wanted to shout out, "Hey, but I'm a Christian." But none of that mattered.

About a year later I left my old company for a better job. My first week was full of boring paperwork and training films.

During a break I ran across the street to the convenience store for a soda and some chips. When I walked into the store, I noticed everyone stopped and stared at me. I thought maybe they had mistaken me for Walter Payton or somebody else famous. (Some white people can't tell black men apart, you know. I've been mistaken for a lot of different people in the past.) After finding the items I wanted I approached the counter to pay for them. I gave my money to the middle-aged woman behind the counter. She glared at me like I had stolen her new big-screen television. She gathered my change, and as I reached for it, she threw it on the counter and looked away. I thought to myself, *What's wrong with her?* I was just about to point out the wrong that had befallen me when I noticed that everyone in the store, including several gentlemen, were standing behind me, staring. Wisdom prevailed, and I gathered my scattered coins and proceeded back to my office.

Once safely inside the office, I told my manager about the situation that had just occurred. He calmly asked me, "Don't you know where you are?"

I said, "Yes, in Chicago."

He replied, "Don't you know what neighborhood you're in?" He saw my confusion and continued, "This is Marquette Park. This is the neighborhood in which Dr. King tried to march and was stoned."

All at once those black-and-white news clips came to mind. I became temporarily pained by the prospects of being stoned myself. And, once again it didn't matter if I had a degree or if I had seen Jesus in person. The statement was clear: "Stay with your own kind."

When I became a Christian, I was taught that I was part of a family in which age, race, or economic standing didn't matter. I even bragged to my brothers about my new family. I told them that wherever I went, there would be people who loved me even though they didn't know me.

I later had to apologize for my ignorant boasts.

I never want to be found guilty of putting everyone of a particular race under the same banner just because of his or her skin color. It would be indeed foolish and sinful to accuse an entire race of people of the same insensitivity, sin, and fears. For I understand how it feels to be judged by my race. Every time I'm pulled over and questioned by a policeman for being somewhere he thinks I shouldn't be, I understand the feeling. Each time a white woman grips her purse tightly as I walk near, I understand. When the same woman screams to her young child as I come near, "Jimmy, come here quickly," I understand. Each time a security guard follows me around a store even though I may be wearing a great suit and tie with plenty of hard-earned cash in my pockets, I understand. Every time it is assumed I'm a bellboy, janitor, cook, or some other form of hired help, I understand the feeling. And no! I don't sing, dance, rap, slam dunk, or shine anyone's shoes but my own. While these are all honorable and honest livelihoods, they are not mine.

A painfully recent survey showed that over half of non-blacks in the United States believed that African Americans are less intelligent than whites, less patriotic, more violence-prone; more likely to "prefer to live on welfare," and less likely to "prefer to be self-supporting."

The misunderstandings go both ways. I know that we should judge people by their own merits, and not on the merits of their race. Yet it took years and many experiences for me to judge white people on their individual performances. I never actually knew anyone white until college except for some of my school teachers. Most of them kept their personal distance, and that was fine with me. My prejudice toward whites, then, was a reaction to their almost constant negative reaction to my presence in "their" world.

But when I was saved and freed from sin, I honestly believed things would be different. I had a whole new cast of family and friends to enjoy and get to know.

One of them was a guy on campus named Nick. Nick was a self-described "military brat." He played a folk guitar and loved the Lord. While many of his friends were uncomfortable around me and my kind, Nick was always an example of God's love in flesh. We spent many hours talking about our Lord and His will for our lives. I think of him often.

And then there was Pastor Fred Luthy and his wife. They were the pastors of the local Lutheran church in Big Rapids. They befriended all the young people involved in the Youth Ambassadors. It never mattered to them that we were all black. Pastor Luthy was more concerned about us as people and about where we were coming from than with the novelty that black students were coming to his church. He gave us the chance to join in his congregation's life. For instance, he asked us to teach his congregation some of the songs from the black gospel tradition. It seemed odd to us to sing those songs in midwestern Lutheran services. (I'm sure it expanded the horizons of many Big Rapids Lutherans, too.) Pastor Luthy even focused some of the church Bible studies on problems we were facing. We felt very blessed to be counted that important in his eyes.

Pastor Luthy didn't stop with formal activities either. He and his wife welcomed us—a bunch of homesick black students who often felt out of place in small-town Michigan—into their home. We'd play board games and eat Mrs. Luthy's great cooking. They spent countless hours counseling us, or simply providing a haven for us. Many other Christians in town tried to "evangelize" us without really finding out who we were. The Luthys made the investment of time and hospitality to offer us a home away from home.

I believe that's the difference between a "formula" approach to racial reconciliation and the heart of the biblical mandate that says to love one another, period: the willingness to be someone's home away from home. Pastor Luthy's love and pastor's heart have always been an example of unselfishness to me.

Unfortunately, these few and a handful of others are the only white people who would count as heroes in my life. I wish I could testify of numerous brothers and sisters of European descent who stood next to the countless numbers of black heroes that have touched my life. But, the roll is short indeed. Should you happen to be Caucasian I'm almost positive the same can be said about those African American heroes on your roster. The fact of the matter is we've done a lousy job of being heroes for Christ in this country.

I believe we were given the perfect opportunity in this country to show the world the love of Jesus Christ—and we blew it. The year was 1968. Everything seemed to change overnight. The assassinations of Robert Kennedy and Martin Luther King seemed to bring an end to the Civil Rights Movement. It was now legal for blacks to vote in every state. Countless uncivilized laws had been changed to allow all of us in this country equal access under the law. While I understand laws are only rules set to govern the actions of men and they in no way can legislate the condition of the heart, it was indeed a God-sent start.

While much of society was taking a "wait and see" attitude on civil rights, there were others who were bound and determined not to live an integrated life. They moved their companies and families to the suburbs. They actually started new communities in which they made sure people of different colors were not allowed. Many real estate agents acquired millions of dollars by spreading vicious rumors and stirring up the fears and hate of whites. "You'd better sell your home before it's too late. You don't want *them* moving in next door to you. One of *them* may marry your daughter or son."

While the world panicked, God was giving the church an opportunity to be the example He spoke about in His word. John 13:34–35 says, "A new command I give you: Love one another. As I have loved you, so you must love one another. By this all men will know that you are my disciples, if you love one another." If racial reconciliation and brotherly love were ever going to work, they had to work in the late sixties. But they didn't.

It was indeed legal and "respectable" for us to walk together, to live together, to vote together, and to worship together. But we decided to go our separate ways. Most of the white churches who occupied the cities pulled up their pulpits and moved to the suburbs. They abandoned beautiful historical buildings, selling them to congregations of color. Dr. King's famous statement of the early sixties is still true: "Sunday morning is the most segregated time of the week in the United States of America." We let our opportunity pass with hardly a tear being shed.

Just as God called Jonah to preach to the wicked city of Nineveh, so has God called the church to arise and go to the cities, suburbs, and farms of this country and cry against the wickedness of prejudice, hate, and racism. But the church has said, "No." It has spent millions of dollars to leave the city and get away from people who are different. In fact, the church has so divided itself that it does not and cannot represent Christ's body. God never sent half a prophet to do a whole prophet's job. By refusing to worship or have any real significant relationships across the color barriers, we have turned the body of Christ into a mutation.

We know what happened to Jonah when he disobeyed God's call and fled on a ship. He sent a great wind on the sea and stirred up a terrible storm. I believe God is sending a similar warning to the church in our country. The winds of change, the storms of riots, lootings, and crime are saying to us, "Turn around and fulfill your destiny."

Too often, though, we leave the experts to solve the problems. In Jonah's case, the experts were the sailors. They knew enough to throw the cargo into the sea to lighten the ship. They were used to rough water and storms. *But there was something about this storm that caused a panic.* They called on their skills and were unable to right the boat. Likewise, we live in a society where the experts are perplexed. Nothing the experts try today is really working. They are calling on their gods and not being delivered. The gods of money, power, position, and prestige are all incapable of saving society.

But Jonah, the person who had the key to calming the storm, had gone below deck to sleep. Where is the church today? While the world is looking for an answer, the church is sleeping through the storm. We're sleeping at our conferences and all the other special things we do to keep ourselves entertained.

The story goes on to tell how the sailors cast lots to find out who was responsible for the storm. As you well know, the lot fell on Jonah, not on the "pagan" sailors. We have been taught that only sinners upset God. We are being told every day that the sinners in our society are the reason for the decay of our country. We say it's their fault that our morals have slipped to an all-time low. But they are *supposed* to sin. That's why they are called "sinners"! Nothing a person does should surprise us if he or she doesn't have a relationship with Christ. But as was the case with Jonah, we the church must realize that the lot often falls on us. It is *we* who are to be light to a dark land. *We* are at fault, not the sinners.

Jonah told the sailors that he was a Hebrew who worshiped the Lord, the maker of heaven and earth. In the same way, when the world asks us Christians who we are, we begin to brag about our relationship with God. We tell everybody about our church and the wonderful choirs we have. We show off our degree from the Bible college we've attended. Finally, after the bows have been taken and the world is impressed, they ask the question the sailors posed to Jonah: "What have you done?" (Jonah 1:10).

What have we done to make God so angry? Why have we ignored His voice to the point that He has to get our attention in a way that makes the world call us hypocrites?

As the storm raged on, the sailors turned to Jonah and asked, "What should we do to you to make the sea calm down for us?" (Jonah 1:11).

"Pick me up and throw me into the sea," Jonah replied, "and it will become calm. I know it is my fault that this great storm has come upon you" (Jonah 1:12).

Read it again: Jonah knew that this storm was his fault, a direct result of his disobedience to God. Like Jonah, we must take some responsibility for the shape our country is in. Jonah knew what God wanted from him. He explained to the sailors, "It's my fault; just throw me overboard." Their reaction was predictable. "Instead, the men did their best to row back to land. But they could not, for the sea grew even wilder than before" (Jonah 1:13). The "experts" heard what Jonah said would calm the sea, but they decided to try their own way. Still, nothing they did worked.

As humankind tries to defy the will of God, it is confounded by the power He displays. Experts all over our great land have used their collective reasoning to suggest how to end the distress and turmoil. No matter how hard they try, however, it is to no avail. The weather became worse as the sailors fought the waves. Likewise, I believe things in America will become worse until we bow to God's will. We cannot go along with society when God is calling us another way.

After Jonah was thrown overboard the raging sea grew calm. After the storm had accomplished its mission, it was over. Many storms in our lives are just there to get our attention. Much of what churches are suffering today is just a wake-up call. Many congregations enjoy the best of music. They have beautiful buildings with comfortable seats. Their pastors are well-educated and decorated with degrees and honors. But the young people aren't convinced that the message is real. They sleep around and experiment with drugs, often following the examples set by their elders. In other words, there is nothing happening in the hearts of the congregation.

So what happens next? In the story, Jonah was swallowed by a great fish. Most people look at the fish prepared by God to swallow Jonah as some kind of monster. On the contrary, the fish enabled Jonah to survive. Left in the sea, he would have certainly perished. To be sure, being inside the fish wasn't comfortable. There were no cushioned pews or harmonizing choirs. The man of God was alone and uncomfortable. I'm sure the men on the boat thought he was dead and his God had forsaken him.

Listen, now: *We, too, are experiencing a deliverance.* God has prepared a vessel of deliverance to get us back on track. And that vessel is the church.

The world is saying that the church is dead. They say the church is ineffective and out of step. But in reality God is allowing us an opportunity to make a comeback.

Like Jonah in the fish, we cry and complain about what is happening to us. How uncomfortable it is to be stuck in situations that we cannot control! But maybe God is trying to deliver us or our congregations. The fish may not be comfortable, but at least we are still alive.

Inside the fish, Jonah cries out to God. One of his statements echoes through history to our shores: "Those who cling to worthless idols forfeit the grace that could be theirs" (2:8). Those who hold on to old idols, prejudices, and hatred will forfeit the grace of God in their lives just as surely today as in Jonah's time. As Jonah repents, though, he praises God for rescuing him from the depths of the sea, and he acknowledges God's mighty power. As a result, God commands the fish to spit Jonah onto dry land. The church can only be completely free when God speaks to our situation and says, "Let them go." I also believe if God is the author of our deliverance, He will set us down on "dry land."

In a display of His marvelous grace, the word of the Lord came to Jonah a second time: "Go to the great city of Nineveh and proclaim to it the message I give you" (Jonah 3:2). The word of the Lord came after all that Jonah had done to run away from

God's call. It came after all the hatred and bigotry Jonah displayed. It came after Jonah paid to leave the place God had desired him to be. It came after Jonah repented inside the belly of the great fish that God had prepared for his deliverance. After all the time he wasted running and denying the very God who made him the great man he was, God spoke to Jonah "a second time."

I believe God is speaking to His church today a second time. He is saying, "Love one another." It doesn't matter what the color of the person is; the world is looking for an example of something that works. God never said the world would know His disciples by their buildings, degrees, programs, or beautiful robes. He said they would know we were Christians because of the love we would have for one another.

Nineveh was restored because Jonah finally did what he should have done in the first place. He walked into the city and displayed the love of God by preaching to people he had hated before.

After Jonah repented, he had less time to get the job done that he'd been called to do. Things in Nineveh had grown worse because of his delay. The church today must understand that we, too, have less time than before. And yes, things are worse than they were thirty years ago. But God is saying to us, "Jonah, you *still* have to go to the city."

The body of Christ today has the same mandate as Jonah. God is calling the whole body to walk into our cities, suburbs, rural areas, and reservations and, as a complete body, proclaim the Gospel. We have been sending a portion of the body to do a whole body's job. If Jonah's arm had gone to Nineveh alone, the job would never have been completed. Maybe a few people would have gotten the message if his head had rolled into town by itself and preached the Word, but the entire people would not have repented.

While we have some individual heroes in the evangelical movement, they alone are not enough. While there are a few teachers and lay people who demonstrate the love of Christ across racial lines, they alone are not enough. God is calling the entire cavalry to arms. The effectiveness of the Gospel message will shine through only when the majority of us believe it enough to live it.

Here's your chance to be a hero. Somebody is waiting for you.

9

Ain't Got a Clue

Like the blind we grope along the wall,
feeling our way like men without eyes.
At midday we stumble as if it were twilight;
among the strong we are like the dead.
(Isaiah 59:10)

EVERY JOURNEY IS filled with many twists and turns. The destination may be the same, but the scenery will change along the way. My journey during the late seventies and early eighties was filled with many twists and turns, as well as highs and lows.

In 1977 I married my college sweetheart. The following year I became the father of a beautiful little girl named Chane Latrice. The three of us lived in a small two-bedroom apartment on the south side of the city, in a section of Chicago known as South Shore. Our neighborhood was full of apartment buildings tightly packed together. We were only two blocks from Lake Michigan. The summers were cool and breezy, and the winters were miserably cold. "How miserable was it?" you may ask. It got so cold on our apartment grounds that one wintry day I discovered my car battery had cracked in half due to the bitter wind and temperature. *That's* how miserably cold it was.

Marriage, as many of you know, is not the easiest institution in which to achieve success. But we were bound and determined to do so. We were twenty-year-olds in a new city, and we hardly knew each other. We had some things in common as married couples should—one of which, I pray, is not something most couples should have in common. Her father had been shot to death when she was a little girl. How many couples do you know that can say each had a parent shot to death? Believe me, it's not something upon which to build a relationship. But I could certainly understand my wife's pain as she spoke about losing her father and what that did to her.

My first job was an assistant manager of a pharmacy chain. Even so, I wanted to use my degree in commercial art. I applied at countless agencies and corporations that ran ads in the paper. Unfortunately, I was never offered a job, and I began to believe I had wasted those years in school on a career that was leading nowhere.

Finally, I was introduced to a young lady at Johnson Publishing Company. Johnson produces *Ebony* and *Jet* magazines, among other great media products. I was excited about the prospect of working with them. They gave me a great tour of their facilities and treated me as if they really appreciated my talents. Although they didn't have any openings at that time, they did offer me a freelance artist position for *Ebony Jr.* The offer just didn't work out with my working schedule, and I declined. That was the only time in three years I was offered any kind of job in commercial art. Even though I never worked for them, for years I bragged that Johnson Publishing Company made me an offer, but I had to turn them down.

My son Jerald Jr., to whom I quickly gave the nickname "J.R.," was born on September 10, 1979. September 10 was also Granddaddy's birthday. No longer was I just Jerald; I was also "Daddy." I loved every bit of it. My son and daughter gave me another reason to keep going. No matter what anyone else thought of me, my kids still loved me. When the money got tight, they still looked at me like I was the king of the world. When I walked in the door after a long day they always ran or crawled to meet me with big bright smiles and hugs and kisses to match. They believed I could do anything. And there were days that I felt they were right.

As the years passed my ministry and career life took the usual paths. Over a six-year period I went from one job to another. As soon as I got comfortable with a working situation, occupational tragedy would strike. Layoffs, downsizing, and the occasional crazy boss kept me feeling I would never find a long-term, stable, enjoyable job. Many companies felt great about my resume. I did wonderfully on telephone interviews, but I seemed to have problems with the real thing.

Finally, I landed a job with a very large corporation. I spent several years as a representative in their educational division. My first manager, a gentleman from Boston, told me one day, "Jerald, you're the right kind of black guy to move up in our company. You're not too dark, you're a family man, and you get along well with everybody." ("Everybody" to this man meant "even white people.") For a year and a half he appeared to be right. I received two promotions, and it seemed as though I would keep climbing the good old corporate ladder. That is, until I reached a level that I could not pass. For the first time I was going to meet the "glass ceiling"—that invisible barrier that cannot be named in polite company, but keeps you from advancing any further. When I hit it, I hit it really hard.

I had worked diligently for almost three years to get my dream job: a field position that would allow me to showcase my talents outside of our offices. The job called for an outgoing person who had experience in our particular field of expertise. When it became available, I applied along with another co-worker, who also happened to be black. We knew the position would go to one of us. I felt confident that I would beat the other gentleman out. Why shouldn't I have been confident? I was the "right kind" of black guy.

As the announcement about the appointment drew near, my manager called both of us into the office to discuss it. She had replaced my original boss and was a lady with plenty of class and sensitivity. Consequently, she wanted to give us the news before we heard it through the grapevine. She told us that neither one of us had received the job; it had been given to a retired

Chicago policeman who had applied through an ad that had been placed in the paper.

After the other gentleman left the office I asked her, "How could they choose someone who was not even an employee?" She confided in me that it had nothing to do with our qualifications. The upper managers simply did not feel that a black man would fit the profile they wanted for this highly visible position.

The color thing was rearing its ugly head. The guy who got the job had no history with our company. He hadn't put any time in like I had. But, once again, that didn't matter. His skin was white, so he got the job.

During these years of employment bliss, I maintained my work in the ministry. There was even one time that I ventured into the ministry as a full-time evangelist. I felt that since the secular jobs were not working out, God might be calling me into full-time ministry. Things went well initially with two or three preaching engagements coming my way each month. But they didn't come in that consistently for long. The calls slowed down pretty quickly—and so did the money. Soon we were rationing food just to feed the children.

Finally, I was called to speak at a church for their Sunday morning service. It was a small black congregation of about one hundred worshipers. The church itself was a Pentecostal group associated with a well-known denomination. I felt extremely honored to be asked to speak anywhere on a Sunday morning; it is truly an expression of trust for pastors to offer their Sunday morning pulpit time to guest speakers. I prepared fervently for this opportunity to speak before these precious souls. As the time drew near to stand in the pulpit and declare God's Word, I felt confident in Him.

I had to borrow a car to get to the church. Mine had given up the ghost about a month earlier. A sister from our church let me borrow her powder-blue Maverick. The car was in bad shape. It was very loud and leaned to one side. But once again I remembered my grandfather's words, "A messed-up ride is better than a dressed-up walk." So I took a messed-up ride to Harvey, Illinois, a small town just south of Chicago.

The service was lively, with great music and testimonies. However, I sensed there were some people there who were just going through the motions. They were used to the sway of the choir and the roar of the organ. They knew when to say "amen" and when to clap their hands. The message God had placed upon my heart had to be just right to shake them out of their rut into spiritual reality. Thank God, it was. The message was blessed, and so was the altar call. God's Spirit rained down on that small church, and when I took my seat I was amazed at what God had done.

As is the tradition of many churches, the pastor rose to receive an offering for me. Many of God's servants rely on the goodness of their congregations for their very survival. I myself had been taught to be sensitive to the needs of those who have given their lives and talents to the service of God, and on this particular Sunday I was praying that the congregation also would be sensitive to my needs. I never told anyone that I was broke. The pastor never asked me how much money I needed, but the Lord knew.

The congregation brought their offerings to the front of the church and placed it in the basket. I could see the basket from where I was seated in the raised pulpit. The amount looked to be double of the regular offering. I thought, *Thank you, Jesus.* The congregation was indeed grateful for what they had heard.

When the service was over, the pastor asked me to wait in the dining hall until he greeted the remainder of the congregation as they left. He seemed to take a long time after most of the congregation was gone. I figured they were counting the money in the treasurer's office and wanted to get it ready for me.

I looked around. The church was clean and well kept. But I knew by the looks of things that they were struggling financially. I decided that if I got only half the offering that would be okay with me. I was preparing to tell the pastor that when he finally came out of a back room.

Walking me to the front door, he told me how blessed my sermon was. He continued with some rambling conversation as we reached the door. We walked through the door and were greeted by bright sunlight. Then he finished his speech by saying, "Brother January, you're a young man. You have a long way to go. The church needs this money. I'm not going to give you any of this. Maybe next time the offering will go to you." With those final words he stepped back quickly, gently pushed me forward, and closed the door—all in one graceful motion. As I heard the lock turn, I suddenly realized he wasn't joking. I stood outside of that church and felt like someone had just stabbed me through the heart. With my sweat-soaked shirt clinging to me and my Bible in my hand, I stumbled back to the borrowed Maverick that sat alone at the curb.

To this day I don't know how I made it home. The gas tank was past the empty mark before I got to church. (I guess you really *can* drive on fumes.) On my way home I struggled with the explanation I would give to my wife. I didn't know how we would feed the children that week. With all the uncertainty the day brought, I was sure of one thing: I would never again depend on the church to sustain me. I love the ministry and the rewards of revived and reborn souls. But I decided on that really messed-up ride home that I would always have a regular job to support my family.

Still, I continued my church work on a volunteer basis. Most of the time, I worked with youth, because that was where my heart was. The young people themselves made those hours of ministry worth it. From basketball leagues to Bible studies, my time with them was extremely rewarding.

Along with youth work came an occasional opportunity to preach, and from those speaking engagements I gained a certain degree of notoriety. God honored His word and the opportunities to minister grew.

In my ministry I had the opportunity to meet some fabulous people, one of whom was Frank Jackson. Frank was a local Christian media celebrity at the time. He was a regular on television and radio and had a very large following. When we met, I was trying to tell him how much I admired him when he stopped me. "I've heard of you before," he said. "Some of the kids you've been working with have told me about you."

We discovered later that we had already met four years earlier at Ferris State when he had visited our group with another minister. Frank invited me to his radio show, and eventually I became his co-host. His belief in me led me to start my own radio and television shows. Through Frank's example, I gained a great understanding of what it took to be prepared for a broadcast. Needless to say, Frank also showed me what professionalism was all about. Today I try to emulate Frank when I'm working with young people who have potential.

As the ministry and occupational wheels kept turning, my personal life was grinding to a halt. My wife and I were growing farther and farther apart, but we had nonetheless been blessed with another beautiful daughter. Charlene Denise, our youngest, was born after our relationship had become quite strained. We both had hoped Charlene's birth might keep us together. But as time went on even the children were not enough to keep our marriage alive.

I found myself living in two separate worlds. In the public eye we were the perfect family. We'd even moved to a cute little house in the suburbs. But within the confines of my own home, things were quite different than in the Sunday morning church hour.

Those days brought me the biggest struggle of my life. When I rose to preach or when I announced the next record over the air, I put on a mask that would not allow anyone to see or hear the hurt inside me. There were days I just didn't want to go home anymore, and yet I would preach about how God could right any wrongs.

Soon after I moved out of our house, we were divorced. I don't blame my ex-wife. I asked her to marry me. I don't blame my children. They are God's gift to me, and I love them more than my next breath. I blame myself, just like thousands of you who have gone through broken relationships. It's not important who started what; the fact was it was finished. Some men might feel I should have been happy for the chance to start all over. To be free to test the singles market probably made me the envy of a lot of guys. But to me being divorced was like going through the death of a close friend.

I found myself taking long, lonely walks that led nowhere. I probably saw more movies in the first six months of separation than in my entire life prior to that time. My appetite disappeared. People wanted to know what kind of great diet I was on. I lost nearly thirty pounds in less than two months. But I was in no mood to celebrate.

I was living the ultimate contradiction. How could I keep on preaching and ministering to people, especially the young people whom I encouraged to always wait on God to lead them to the right mate? I had told them how I waited until I was married to have sex. I explained to them that was the way God planned it. "You should have sex and children only in wedlock," I would say. "That's the way God planned it. I waited until marriage to have sex with the right person: my wife, and only my wife. So wait on God to help you find the right mate!" These young people were looking to me to be their example of how to find God's will for their lives, and I was letting them down. "A child should be raised by his father and mother," I'd preach. But I wasn't living with my own children anymore.

There I was in the big city, experiencing some occupational success, ministerial success, and media success. In the midst of all that success, I had become part of the ultimate failure. My life seemed to mirror the world I lived in. I became as confused as many of those who shared that world with me.

Finally, I had to turn to God for the clues to find my place again. And I've had to *stay* before God to make sense of what I've seen since.

There were, and are, people in the church who have all the opportunities in the world without taking advantage of them. The answers seem as simple as the nose on our faces, and yet we can't figure it out. Going from congregation to congregation, I had the opportunity to meet some outstanding men and women of God. These people from my own community of color showed a tremendous ability to make it against the odds. With God's help, they made dollars stretch far beyond their original monetary value. With churches and facilities that were many times substandard, they made miracles happen on a weekly basis. The church has been, and continues to be, the strength and stability of the urban African-American community.

However, there has been a conspiracy of silence concerning our own shortcomings. With all the talents, resources, visions, and dollars that are born, raised, and fed into our communities, we are just not seeing a return on our investment. We have allowed jealousy, pride, excuses, and lethargy into our neighborhoods along with the countless numbers of drug dealers and other garden varieties of crooks. While our families have become victims in their own homes, we stand by and give excuses for our lack of action. Now that we have the freedom and resources to control our destinies, we too often sit on our Bibles blaming whites for our problems.

Yes, I do agree that our country has a problem with racial prejudice. Blacks in many cases have been shunned, exploited, or abused by whites. But that's a sorry excuse when you look at the way we've dropped the ball ourselves. We've created and learned plenty of good things over the years, but many of our leaders have become good at begging as well. "Standing with our hand out, looking for a handout" has become the way of life for many.

Since God opened the doors of freedom in this country for us, we have taken advantage of it. Most of us could cite thousands of great examples to prove that fact. We now have the right to vote, to ride in the front of the bus, and to attend the schools of our choice. Millions of African Americans have benefited from the labors of those who marched, prayed, and conducted strikes, and from the pain of those who were jailed, beaten, burned out, and turned out. Every time I walk through a door these courageous men and women have opened, I am honoring them.

My grandparents taught us when we were children, "Not everybody is your friend." They would tell us, "You can't trust everybody you meet." That advice has served me well. But they also taught us to trust God and to give people a chance to prove themselves as friends. This advice was normal for young people to receive in years past. The old folks passed their wisdom and dignity on to the younger generation.

But something went terribly wrong.

During those years when God was making it possible for us to overcome, we had no problem worshiping Him. There were times no one listened to us but God. Through suffering and affliction, our ancestors built an intimate relationship with the God of the universe. But now we have thrown away our relationship to God. While I used to see dozens of young people in our church every Sunday, now fewer and fewer youths attend. Too often parents quit coming to church when their children grow up. And many of their grown-up children say, "My parents *made* me come to church. I'm not going to do that with *my* children." That makes three generations dodging church.

Just like the children of Israel, we have forgotten the God Who brought us over. Yes, I know we turn out in droves for "The Three Big Sundays": Easter, Mother's Day, and Christmas. But people's being selectively religious has never impressed God. Because of our tendency to turn our backs on God, we find ourselves wondering what has gone wrong. We can vote, but very few of us do. We can ride in the front of any bus we want, but most of our young people choose to ride in the back. We can go to school all day every day, but our young people are dropping out of school at a record pace. We have teens and young adults who can rap at a rate of 500 words per second, but they can't read at even a fifth-grade level.

The fault lies directly at our feet. And before you get upset with what you are reading, please take a moment and look at the facts.

The facts are: The leading cause of death among black youth is homicide. Eighty percent of victimized African Americans are victimized by other blacks. Six million black males are in prison while only 400,000 black males are in college. One-fourth of all black males between the ages of sixteen and thirty are in prison. Two-thirds of all black children come from single-mother homes. Fifty percent of all black teens are unemployed.

It's hard to argue with the facts. What was previously done to us by others is now being done to us by ourselves. What's the answer? I believe it's right in front of us.

When I was in the eighth grade, I was introduced to algebra. I had done well in math until that point and looked forward to learning all I could about the new forms of math. There were simple formulas to follow that would lead me to a quick and correct answer if I did them correctly. But for some reason "A + B = C" never made sense to me. Needless to say, I failed the class. Even though I had a teacher who knew how to teach the course and a book with all the directions, I didn't have a clue.

We live in a society to which God has given simple formulas. Those formulas, if followed, will lead to the answers in life. But "folks just ain't got a clue."

A clue is simply anything that guides or directs us in the solution of a problem or a mystery. According to Isaiah 59, the people of Israel had a problem that needed a solution. They needed God to deliver them from the problems that plagued their community.

Do I really need to list the problems that plague our community today? What can I tell you about drugs, gangs, genocide, teen and unwed pregnancies, hopelessness, and unfaithfulness that you don't already know? The list goes on and on, of course. Our problems are as great as those that plagued the children of Israel.

In Isaiah's time, the people had gone on a fasting and prayer campaign, but there was no deliverance. "'Why have we fasted,' they say, 'and you have not seen it? Why have we humbled ourselves, and you have not noticed?'" (Isaiah 58:3). Evidently, these people were accustomed to hearing from God when they called, because He had delivered them many times in the past.

But God was not answering the line on this occasion, and He had His reasons. "Yet on the day of your fasting you do as you please and exploit all your workers. Your fasting ends in quarreling and strife, and in striking each other with wicked fists. You cannot fast as you do today and expect your voice to be heard on high" (Isaiah 58:3–4).

Our great nation has grown accustomed to enjoying God's favor and deliverance. Just look back into our history, and the role of God can be seen. Our victories in World Wars I and II certainly show God's favor to our country. And God certainly delivered my people from slavery and blessed their work in the civil rights movement. Curiously, though, after all the times He has delivered us throughout history, God seems to be deaf to many of our cries today.

The people in Isaiah's day were angry at God and blamed Him for not keeping His word to them. But, as is the way with God, He sent His prophet—in this case, Isaiah—to "clue them in."

When the people asked Isaiah, "What is wrong with God?" he told them: "Surely the arm of the Lord is not too short to save, nor his ear to dull to hear" (Isaiah 59:1). In other words, the problem was not with God. He was willing to help, and His hearing worked quite well, thank you. Isaiah went on to say, "But your iniquities have separated you from your God; your sins have hidden his face from you, so that he will not hear" (Isaiah 59:2). The problem is and was with His people. Those people He had invested in over the generations were now the same ones accusing Him of not keeping His word. Many were saying He wasn't real, that He was just a figment of their forefathers' imaginations.

When I hear people today with similar arguments, I cringe at the thought of what God's answer must be to us. There is already a natural gulf between God and men. Jesus Christ closes that gap when we receive Him unconditionally into our hearts as Savior. But our salvation does not give us license to sin continually and wave it in God's face.

Isaiah said, in essence, "Your sins have kept good things from you." The problem with Isaiah's audience was that they "did religion" through a fasting and prayer campaign, but at the same time they kept on sinning. Our Christian culture is good at having campaigns and conferences. There are annual, biannual, once in a while, and whenever-we-feel-like-it types of events. We have meetings and conferences to serve all types of needs. Some of these gatherings have even proven to honor God. However, many of these "Gospel tea parties" just serve as occasions for men and women to show off the latest fashions.

They ain't got a clue.

Isaiah explained to the people that God turned His face from them because of their many sins, any one of which was enough to separate them from God's goodness. "For your hands are stained with blood, your fingers with guilt. Your lips have spoken lies, and your tongue mutters wicked things" (Isaiah 59:3). In addition, God pointed out that no one spoke up for what was right. "No one calls for justice" (Isaiah 59:4). No one stood up for righteousness. No one complained about the violation of God's law.

It has been a national tragedy that so many of our leaders have remained silent for so long about the condition of our community. Only now when we're at a crisis point has it become stylish to speak out on black-on-black crime. If the Klan or some other group was killing black boys the way we are killing each other, we would have been screaming for justice years ago. But our silence has been deafening. For thousands who have died, our cries are too late.

"No one pleads his case with integrity," the prophet continues (Isaiah 59:4). Not only do we have a deficit of leaders who call for the administration of what is just, correct, and proper, the leaders we do have often are lacking in integrity.

The absence of wholeness and fairness has to be evident to plead a winnable case against injustice. The Rodney King beating and the first verdict that followed were tragic. I'm filled with anger and pain every time I replay the incident in my mind. Don't worry about his past or his future, he was still treated wrong. Someone has to pay for that kind of crime.

I know it could well have been me being stomped and beaten by the very people who are sworn "to protect and serve" us. The reactions of people all over this country were understandable, and no one cried louder in our community than some of those in leadership. That's the way it should have been. I was proud to see so many stand together and come to the rescue of one brother who had been wronged. We must all fight to see that this kind of violation of the law is stopped.

The moment I heard about the riots in L.A. that followed the King verdict, I had a flashback of the Detroit riots I witnessed in my youth. There were similarities between the incidents. Both were sparked by the controversial treatment of a black man at the hands of police. Both laid waste to neighborhoods where people lived and worked.

You see, my memories of Detroit riots aren't from the perspective of a rioter, but of a young person watching his neighborhood change before his eyes. As the events in L.A. unfolded,

I couldn't help but wonder what the young people of L.A. were going through. I prayed for those children. Many of them were asked to take sides and take action when no one was considering what they were going through.

Young people see injustices that provoke angry responses. I know from experience that they get angry, too. But they also understand that when their neighborhood hurts, they hurt.

Given that, shouldn't we cry even louder when we see and hear the daily slaughter of our own people by our own people? We perpetrate the kind of violence that makes the Rodney King beating look like a game of tag. Those of us who don't call it both ways are doomed to a public life that lacks any real integrity.

Isaiah also told the people that "they rely on empty arguments and speak lies" (Isaiah 59:4). People of all colors are making up lies and calling them truth, from those who support homosexual marriages to those who say homosexuals and blacks are all in the same boat. In my view, gay rights and the civil rights movement have about as much in common as George Bush and Louis Farrakhan. They are totally separate issues and should not be mentioned in the same context. I resent the fact that many of my leaders are comparing me and my brothers and sisters to a group of people who only wish to have the right to sleep together. I don't owe homosexuals anything, and they have never done anything in my community except leach off the work and prayers of my forefathers.

I was asked by a well-known white evangelical leader, "Why are black people so unconcerned about the gay agenda? Aren't they concerned about what is happening?"

I informed that leader that most black folks I knew had greater things to be concerned about. I replied, "Most white businessmen don't want to live next door to me. Most white Christians don't want to live next door to me. And white homosexuals aren't breaking down the doors to get into my community either. This isn't *our* problem; it's *yours*."

I truly believe the white church in America is not used to any real persecution. They're afraid of demonstrators who might come into their churches and throw condoms on the parishioners as they listen to a speaker who is giving a biblical view on homosexuality. They're afraid that demonstrators may attack them, spit on them, and call them hateful.

Understand this: homosexuals are also part of the black community, and we know they are there. They are our brothers, sisters, and cousins. We really do love them. They are part of our families. But they'll be among the first to tell you that the ridiculous arguments of the predominantly white gay movement have not and will never hold much water in our community. The rights that were won by my forefathers are much too important to hand over to some individuals who feel they have to legitimize their sexual cravings.

The message is plain. Don't ever say that because you prefer same-sex intercourse you are the same as me. One is skin, the other is sin.

Isaiah 59:5 continues, "They hatch the eggs of vipers and spin a spider's web." The spider's web represents those things that take time and concentration to assemble, but are still weak and insignificant when they are completed. So much of what is held up as representative of God is only spider webs. Something may look good and have tremendous cost and effort invested in it, but still be unable to stand up to a strong wind.

In like manner, the world can see through much of what we call our "clothing of righteousness." Consider the next verse in Isaiah: "Their cobwebs are useless for clothing; they cannot cover themselves with what they make." All our self-righteousness cannot cover our nakedness before God. Romans 13:14 says, "Rather, clothe yourselves with the Lord Jesus Christ, and do not think about how to gratify the desires of the sinful nature." Adam and Eve used leaves to cover themselves, but they still couldn't hide their sin. Let's face the truth: our webs are too thin to be clothes of righteousness. The world can see right through us when we say one thing and do another, and even more, God can see through our webs even when men can't.

Many of these misled, cobweb-clothed individuals are akin to a man standing in a train station with a bus ticket in his hand: no matter how real his ticket may be, he'll never go anywhere with it. In the same way, a form of godliness without the power of God will never result in the kind of blessing that comes from true obedience.

These people were so frustrated over their lack of success with God that they likened themselves to blind men. "Like the blind we grope along the wall, feeling our way like men without eyes. At midday we stumble as if it were twilight; among the strong, we are like the dead" (Isaiah 59:10). Whenever we close our eyes to God's truth, God has the right to shut the way to our peace. That makes the simple things impossible to figure out. We're left without a clue—and the spiritually blind can't see the dangers or blessings surrounding them.

Somehow we must come to grips with the truth that our future is in the hand of God. We must fall on our faces before Him and cry out for His forgiveness and direction. He is waiting.

During the breakdown of my marriage, I turned to God. I was confused and afraid I would never be happy again. One of the ministers who had been supporting me through a time of much counseling and no improvement finally said, "Jerald, I know neither of us believes in divorce. But it may be your option here. That sort of trauma could be fatal to your personal ministry, and I'm advising you now to commit to teach and preach even more while you work through it."

Like my minister said, I didn't believe in divorce. I still dreamed of being a father in a two-parent home, but my wife and I couldn't live together anymore. So after the divorce I took my minister's advice and threw myself more than ever into church work. For some time, the church became more of a home than the empty apartment I'd moved into. I continued to minister to the lost even though there were times I had to rush back to my car before the tears would roll from my eyes. You may not understand it, but God healed me through my ministry.

After the divorce, my children moved with their mother to Alabama. I was a single man again for a while before God allowed me to meet Jerra. Jerra and I were simply good friends for some time. But when I decided to move to Denver in 1985, I asked her to marry me. Jerra has been my wife and best friend for years now. She is a godly woman whose inner beauty is the only thing that shines brighter than her outer beauty. We have two handsome sons, Craig and James, who make our home lively.

I never stopped missing my other children. But God has even worked things out between their mother and me so we can all be a part of one another's lives.

There *are* answers to the problems we face. You can find them in the textbook God has provided for us. God has the answers to those hard-to-figure problems. God has provided teachers to help us proceed on our journey. If we only listen and take heed, we would never have to fail.

10

No Magic Fix

We also rejoice in our sufferings,
because we know that suffering produces perseverance;
perseverance, character; and character, hope.
(Romans 5:3–4)

"I BELIEVE IN everybody. I think we're going to make it. But I know the price."

James Baldwin said that in an interview in the sixties. I don't think he was ever in church ministry, but those statements apply to anyone who works to develop other people.

Ministry, for example, demands a belief that God can work in everybody, and so everybody is worth your time. It demands a positive outlook too. But it also demands a firm grip on reality, and one of the biggest reality checks you'll face in seeking to help someone else succeed as a disciple of Jesus Christ is this: there's a price to pay for the privilege.

There are no "magic fixes" in ministry. There are no step-by-step formulas. You can only develop relationships, act in a trustworthy way, and continually rely on God.

I've found that to be especially true in youth work. My journey took an unexpected turn when I moved to Colorado. For six years, I hardly had a dull moment, because I was holding down as many positions as I could with different youth organizations and churches. At one time, I held seven different youth positions at once. I was trying somehow to make up for Andre's death by influencing as many young people as possible.

Perseverance is one thing. Stupidity is another. I had fooled myself into believing that I was somehow the answer for all the problems young people had, but in reality I was only creating problems for myself and my family. I had to collapse from exhaustion one night before God got my attention. Then He used a brother named Mike to show me I couldn't do it all myself. I needed to face my own mortality and start doing more of God's will for ministry, and less of Jerald's will. I had to repent of my wrong and commit to a more sensible way of living.

You might think this is strange, but once I'd made that decision, I noticed a new depth in my relationships with the kids I encountered. Without the self-imposed worry of having to reach every young person, I could value those kids God allowed me to work with even more. It's made my journey so much richer. For instance, from 1990 through 1992 I was privileged to work in Denver with Mark Pollard, a one-time Urban Director for Youth for Christ. Mark founded a ministry called Common Ground. We were blessed to go into area schools and work with young people who needed positive role models. I say "blessed" because those students taught me more about life in the nineties than any book or course I could have taken. Their love kept me coming back time after time to their schools for the sheer joy of being with them.

During those two years, I volunteered my time with Common Ground and made money through my own marketing company that specialized in culturally sensitive marketing. But the sensitivity I learned from working with the students—especially those from Aurora Hinkley High School—was something that put my marketing sensitivity into perspective. These students weren't clients; they were young men and women that, for some reason, God was allowing me to influence. I learned to look at them as individuals, and I began to realize the God-given value of every one of them.

God taught me to share His love with these kids in a way that wasn't preachy. He allowed me to live the Gospel out by investing time in some of the greatest minds He'd created. For a few of the youth I was like a father or much-needed uncle. I became convinced that the hearts of those kids could someday make a difference in the world.

The more I worked with those students, the more I believed in them. The trick was getting them to believe in themselves. Many of them had lost hope for their futures. Some had little confidence in themselves. Too many had bought into the lie that it was somehow cool to be tasteless, classless, and under-achievers. Some of them were convinced that it wasn't fresh to be smart. Their responses to life were understandable. In their world, it was in style to be abusive to yourself and others. Too many role models were murderers, dope pushers, or whores.

How could I get these kids to trust me? There was no magic formula for reaching these kids, but my wife's famous double-cheese lasagna was one effective ploy. You see, we'd build rela-tionships with some of them by asking them to come over to our house to do their homework. Afterwards, Jerra would often reward their efforts with a great dinner. After a while, in their own time, those students opened up.

I was "the professional," right? In those two years, the Common Ground kids gave me a reeducation on youth and their world. Many of them expressed their feeling of having no options, and their thoughts about giving in to the streets. Jerra and I took the opportunity to show them a different way. It's not that we had anywhere close to 100 percent success, but through the laughter, arguments, and tears we really had moments when we thought things would work out for everybody.

Life isn't that perfect, though. One of our most trying times began late one night with a phone call from one of the girls in the group. She was clearly upset and sounded as though she'd been crying. And then she gave me the message I'd hoped I'd never hear: one of her friends had been shot.

It was a long night. The girl who had been shot—I'll call her Charese—had been an occasional visitor to Common Ground sessions, but she'd communicated her dream clearly: she want-ed to be an entertainer someday. And Charese had the personality, looks, and smile to make it happen. But like thousands of young people each year in our country, Charese never had the chance to see what life held for her. She died the next day. She was only sixteen years old.

As a minister, I've attended my share of funerals, but I'll never get used to funerals for young people. Charese's funeral was held at our church. It was filled to capacity, and the mix of school-aged kids there was especially disturbing. Gang members were there in force, openly displaying their colors and loyalties. Many others were obviously uncomfortable being inside a church—they just weren't familiar with the surroundings. One young man even explained to me that he didn't know where to sit. In contrast, there were other students there with Christ in their lives.

Something unusual happened as the service progressed. Many of the young men in attendance were overcome with emotion. Some of them were so overwhelmed they had to be taken from the sanctuary. These were gang members who had demonstrated an incredible veneer of toughness just moments before. Everything about them had seemed to demand respect. But as I watched them in those moments, I was reminded again that there was a side of them they seldom showed: the side just beyond the colors, sagging pants, and long, uncombed hair— the side where their hearts were broken. For all the show, these young men were not yet used to death.

At the end of the service, Mark Pollard offered an invitation to receive Christ. Over thirty young people responded, many of whom had been a part of Common Ground sessions. Even under such tragic circumstances, God brought life from death and so assured us that all was not lost.

I learned that it takes time to win the trust of young people. I learned that the only "how-to" book on doing work with urban youth worth using was the Bible. All the others just add variation. I learned that youth have to see your consistency work on their behalf, and there's no substitute for a quality relationship.

That's why I thought I was headed for many more years with Common Ground. I'd come to value their relational approach to ministry, and I was ready to follow through with as many kids as God allowed. But God had other plans.

Mark and I were watching a Monday night football game together when he turned to me and mentioned that Compassion International was looking for a USA Director. My initial reaction was cold; I had no real knowledge of Compassion and their work. But Mark went on to explain that he'd been impressed with Compassion enough to interview with them for the position. Mark had felt the job was not for him, but asked me to consider if God could be leading me that way.

Soon I was on the phone with Dan Brewster, who was serving as acting USA Director along with his regular duties with Compassion's overseas work. I arranged for an appointment. I honestly thought that I'd be "in-and-out" even as I entered Compassion's headquarters for my first interview. *I'll be nice to this Brewster guy and then get the heck out of here*, I thought. *How can I work for a group I know so little about, anyway?*

What I thought would be a simple, one-hour interview turned into over two hours of give and take. Dan explained Compassion's history and philosophy of ministry to children through the church, and expressed his hope—shared by the leaders of Compassion—that Compassion could also offer great things to young people in the United States. I was quickly convinced that Compassion was the next step God had for me. It took four months and twenty-three more interviews, but I finally walked through the headquarter's doors in January 1993 as Compassion's USA Director.

Compassion has given me the opportunity to multiply assistance to young people across this great land of ours. From urban neighborhoods to rural America to Native American reservations, Compassion is dedicated to empowering churches and Christian schools who are committed to the development of children in the United States. Many local ministries and leaders who have a heart for their communities' youth find their efforts crippled from a lack of funding. Compassion comes alongside them and, through funding and some "how-to's" of program development and administration, empowers them to conduct more effective outreach.

Partner support is sometimes used to keep a facility's doors open so children will know it's "the place to go" for safe recreation. Sometimes the support is used for reference material and snacks needed for tutoring sessions that will help children make the most of their education. Funding can even provide more workers dedicated to serving youth through a local church outreach program.

I've taken the opportunity to talk with scores of those workers in the past few months. They're well aware of the lessons I've learned over the years, and that from their own experience. Let me say it again: when you begin to work with young people, you can't just "talk the talk," you have to have an ongoing relationship with those young people that clearly shows the way to the ultimate empowerment: a personal relationship with Jesus Christ.

As you develop relationships with the youth God has allowed you to serve, you must persevere long enough to really get to know those young people, and to allow them to know you. You have to appreciate who, what, and where they are in life to encourage them to do the same for you. Don't try to remake them in your image. Let them come as the old hymn encourages, "Just as I Am."

There's a price to pay if we're going to help our youth make it. Each day I'm consumed with the work of finding ways to help young people. God has a strange way of guiding our footsteps, and though I would have never guessed He'd lead me this way, I'm glad He did.

Part 4
Reflections

Jerald, Jeff, Johnny, and Keith in front of Granddaddy's Bonneville—years before it became a "messed-up ride."

Jerra and I out on the town!

Paul family reunion in 1983. My brothers—Johnny, Jeff, and Keith—and I are in the back row.

11

A Messed-Up Ride or a Dressed-Up Walk

"Lord, if it's you," Peter replied,
"tell me to come to you on the water."
"Come," he said.
(Matthew 14:28–29)

EVERY JOURNEY STARTS with one step. Whether we admit it or not, each one of us is on a journey. Our modes of transportation may be different, but we are all traveling nevertheless.

In December 1955 one woman's action ignited an entire movement. Rosa Parks sat down on a Montgomery city bus that day after a long hard day at work. Her destination was home, the place where she felt most comfortable, respected, and appreciated. For years she had traveled to and from her home, most days by taking a similar seat on a similar bus in Montgomery, Alabama.

Each day Rosa Parks was reminded of the state of society when she deposited her money in the change box in the front of the bus. She then had to exit back through the front door, walk around to the rear door, and then find a seat in the back of the bus. Many times she was forced to stand because there were no seats in the colored section of the bus. Other tired women had gotten on the bus before her and taken all the seats marked for the city's black riders. As she surveyed the bus she would notice empty seats in the front section. But that wasn't supposed to matter to Rosa Parks. Those seats were reserved for passengers who happened to be white.

On one particular December day Sister Rosa had found a seat in the colored section, settled in comfortably, and started her ride home. A white male passenger got on the bus and decided that he wanted to sit where Rosa Parks was sitting. This was a common practice in that day. In fact, it was not uncommon for two black people to give up their seats for one white passenger. But for some reason that December day, this petite woman didn't budge when she was asked by the bus driver to get up. The bus driver told her the bus would not move until she gave up her seat. She sat there anyway. Even when the police were called to arrest her for breaking the law, she never apologized for her actions.

Later when Rosa Parks was asked what type of statement she was trying to make by not moving she simply answered, "I was just tired. I just didn't feel like moving."

Sometimes, all it takes is one person being tired of the status quo to start an entire movement. The Civil Rights Movement didn't start on that day. Dozens of men and women had already stood up for the rights of African Americans and other mistreated people in this land prior to Miss Parks' action. Some had even given their lives.

On May 7, 1955, Reverend George Lee, one of the first black people registered to vote in Humphreys County, used his pulpit and his printing press to urge others to vote. White officials offered Lee protection on the condition he end his voter registration efforts, but Lee refused. He was murdered in Belzoni, Mississippi.

In the same year, Mr. Lamar Smith was shot dead on a courthouse lawn by a white man in broad daylight while dozens of people watched. The killer was never indicted because no one would admit they saw a white man shoot a black man. Mr. Smith had organized blacks to vote in a recent election.

Against the odds and against the wishes of many, a campaign started on December 5, 1955. For more than a year after Rosa Parks's arrest, black people and their friends refused to ride the buses in Montgomery. They encouraged each other with smiles, handshakes, rides, and hopes of a better day. They carpooled, hitchhiked, and walked to work every morning and every evening.

As it had always been, home was their destination. The difference was that they decided to get there on their own terms. It wasn't enough just to be able to ride public buses in Montgomery anymore. The people decided that if they couldn't sit where they wanted to, they wouldn't ride the bus at all. The alternative was difficult for many of them. Sometimes it was downright torture to walk miles to and from work. But a point had to be made.

The rallying point for the Montgomery faithful was the Bible, and they packed out churches on a regular basis to sing and pray. The fuel that kept their effort going was the Spirit of God.

If you've never realized it before, you must understand that the Civil Rights Movement was a spiritual movement. The power that these people called on was not political. They had very few representatives in public office willing to represent their cause. Most of these folks knew that if they called their state capital to talk to their congressman, much less register a complaint, they would be hung up on.

But as the old folks used to say, "I got a telephone in my bosom, and all I got to do is call Him up." Whenever a roadblock came their way, the answer was prayer. When police blocked the entrance to a public building, the answer was prayer. When crowds hassled demonstrators, the answer was prayer. As I researched the history of this time, I was amazed at the role that prayer and faith in God played in the success of the movement.

On November 13, 1956, almost a year after Rosa Parks refused to give up her seat on the bus, the Supreme Court banned segregated seating on Montgomery buses. In December the bus boycott was over, and a new day dawned in Montgomery. Miss Parks could sit wherever she wanted. But more importantly, an example of one person stepping out was documented for the whole world to see.

We live in a society of copycats. Very few people are free thinkers. Even our fashion trends are set by designers. We wait to see what they say we should wear. It's just another glorified form of copying.

We're also infatuated with the "Hollywood Hero" concept. Rambo and his movie action hero buddies make us feel good as they work their magic on the screen. Sometimes, it seems as though we're waiting for a Hollywood hero to step out and, with a few swift karate moves, deal with the problems of our everyday lives.

Real life doesn't work that way, of course. In real life, too many times the hero is missing in action. Very few choose to step out from the crowd and say, "I have to travel another way."

Matthew 14 gives an account of several turning points in the public ministry of Jesus. It tells about the beheading of Jesus' friend and cousin, John the Baptist. It makes note of Jesus wanting to spend some time alone, but then it records His ministry to and feeding of the five thousand who gathered to be near Him. Matthew 14:13 simply says, "When Jesus heard what had happened [John's beheading], he withdrew by boat privately to a solitary place. Hearing of this, the crowds followed him on foot from the towns." Notice that Jesus was not looking for a church service; the church service was looking for Him.

When Jesus stepped out, it was always an event, for Jesus was there to meet the needs of the people. A crowd will always gather when there is something worth gathering for. It really doesn't matter where it is as long as it's where the need is being met. That's why it only helps the church when we open our doors to meet the needs of our communities, whether that need is for a safe place for the children to gather after school or for an adult literacy program. Folks will always hear about a church that is really doing something.

The example of countless individuals of all races who dare to "step out" and make a difference should show us how to change our world. Jesus Christ is the perfect example of one such individual, of course. But my favorite example of someone who "stepped out" in the Bible is Peter. I can relate to Peter's example better because I'm not perfect, and neither was Peter. Maybe you're not perfect either. So the few steps Peter took may speak as an example to you, too. Watch for the contrast in how Jesus and Peter handled the business of "stepping out."

Matthew 14:22 says that after His busy time of ministry, Jesus immediately made the disciples get into the boat and go on ahead of Him while He dismissed the crowd. Consider that carefully: after the disciples were finished distributing food to the people Jesus *immediately* commanded them to leave. In other words, whenever the reason for your ministry is over, you should move on. I can't tell you the number of once-dynamic church outreach programs that, once they have served their purpose, are never allowed to phase out gracefully. When a church hangs on to a formula that worked twenty years ago, it might miss meeting the present needs of the community it's supposed to serve. Change means moving on. Jesus never called us to stand around and take our bows.

Luke 10 tells of how the seventy-two disciples returned to Jesus with joy over their successful public ministry and said, "Lord, even the demons submit to us in Your name." Jesus put it in perspective for them with this response: "Do not rejoice that the spirits submit to you, but rejoice that your names are written in heaven" (verse 20). We have to understand that it really isn't about the gift; it's all about the Giver of the gifts.

According to Matthew 14:23, after Jesus had dismissed the crowd He went up on a mountainside by Himself to pray. Evening found Jesus completing what He originally intended to do. Just a few hours before, Jesus' intention was simply to be alone to pray and reflect on the life of His cousin John. Although His plans had been interrupted by the crowds in need, Jesus kept His purpose in mind. That time by Himself was critical.

More often than not, meeting the needs of others proves to be a schedule-busting proposition. The work of the Kingdom usually doesn't come in sanitary packaging guaranteed to keep you in your safety zone. But I believe God will always give us time to do the things we need to do to keep our lives balanced and in order.

While Jesus was on the mountain, back on the boat the disciples—fresh from a victorious afternoon of healings and miracles—were experiencing a tense night. Just a few hours earlier they were in the limelight with Jesus. Now they were in the darkness of a stormy night being tossed back and forth by the waves.

Where was Jesus? Didn't He know what was going on? Why would He allow some of His choice servants to suffer such discomfort?

Let me suggest to you a common sequence of events in ministry and life. First, *always look for a large trial right after a large victory.* Often a stormy night will follow hot on the heels of a victory. My many years of youth ministry taught me that once a young person is brought into the Kingdom, he or she will usually face a huge trial or temptation. I did. Your faith is often tested right after the biggest win of your life. But don't think God loves you any less in the midst of that challenge, because such things can also help to keep you humble.

Second, understand that *unseen forces will sometimes challenge your journey.* Just as the wind was contrary to the disciples' progress that stormy night, sometimes things you cannot see or understand will work against you. Take heart in those times, because, as the disciples found out, Jesus is never far from you.

Sometime between three and six o'clock in the late night hours (that's the "fourth watch" mentioned in Matthew 14:25), Jesus went out to the disciples. At your darkest hours Jesus has promised to be with you. *And notice, the Scripture says Jesus went out to them.* Sometimes it seems that as we follow God's leading, we are being led into a severe storm. Sometimes that storm takes shape through people misunderstanding each other, or through circumstances you never anticipated. Please don't be distressed in your present situation. If Jesus has truly commanded you to get in the ship, He won't leave you there alone. God was mindful of the disciples, and He is mindful of you. He will come to you.

And He is in control. Many times in Scripture, water represents those things you can see but can't control. Notice that Christ came to the disciples walking on the water. This represents His total control over the water. Jesus controls every situation in which you find yourself.

Even though the disciples had probably assured themselves with the same sort of thoughts as they followed Jesus, when the disciples saw the Lord walking on the lake they were still terrified. "It's a ghost!" they cried out in fear (Matthew 14:26). The disciples were scared because they didn't expect to see Jesus the way they saw Him. But remember that Jesus had told them to go on ahead of Him. That meant He had every intention of being with them that night.

Often we find ourselves doubting the power of God. We say, "Move in my life, Lord!" but the moment He starts moving we get scared. The disciples cried out, "It's a ghost!" Jesus was just doing what God does, and they couldn't handle it, like many church folks today who can't handle the full power of God's Spirit. We're always trying to convince ourselves by saying, "It doesn't take all *that* to change us, does it? God doesn't have to disturb us to move among us, does He?" If it's God, it takes that and a whole lot more. *Let God be God.*

It's no mistake that Jesus immediately said to His disciples, "Take courage! It is I. Don't be afraid" (Matthew 14:27). God has always encouraged His followers to be courageous and not be afraid. Remember Joshua 1:9, my theme verse for life: "Have I not commanded you? Be strong and courageous. Do not be terrified; do not be discouraged, for the LORD your God will be with you wherever you go."

Notice that Jesus had first ministered to the masses. They represent the countless numbers of individuals who understand who Jesus is and want to be touched by Him. But they seldom, if ever, leave the shore. They rarely launch out into the deep with the Lord.

Then there are the twelve who represent the small group of believers who take up their crosses and follow Jesus. More than the "bench warmers," they have a personal relationship with Him.

But the twelve still hadn't stepped out. From the crowded boat came a lone voice. All twelve disciples were on the boat. All of them knew Jesus. They had walked with Him, talked with Him, and been part of His public ministry. But only one called out to Jesus for help to step outside his safety zone.

"Lord, if it's You—" Peter called out. I can imagine him taking a deep gulp of air and swallowing hard before finishing his sentence: "—tell me to come to You on the water" (Matthew 14:28).

Somehow at that moment, Peter realized there was even more to the Lord than he'd discussed with his friends. Maybe Peter was just a blue-collar fisherman, but he was putting together the things he'd seen and heard as he followed Jesus. Jesus had said to the disciples over and over as they watched Him in action, "You can do these things and greater."

Walking on water means stepping outside the boat. It means leaving the familiar and normal. In our context, it means doing the unusual for the hope of the miraculous. When suburban Christians volunteer to serve in the ministry of an inner-city church, they're walking on water. When a young person from the ghetto returns to serve her community after a successful college career that might have led her elsewhere, she's walking on water. When a church agrees that money for ministry to people is better spent than money to redecorate the church foyer, they're walking on water. You get the picture. Still, there are precious few in the United States "church world" who are bold and trusting enough to cry out to God, "Tell me to come out on the water!"

What does it take to make that cry your own?

First of all, *it takes faith in the Lord.* Hebrews 11:6 says, "And without faith it is impossible to please God, because anyone who comes to him must believe that he exists and that he rewards those who earnestly seek him." It's the kind of faith that says, "No matter what society says, I'm stepping out. No matter what my friends say . . . no matter what my choir members say . . . no matter what my homies say . . . I'm stepping out."

Second, *it takes faith in yourself.* It's not the kind of faith that causes some to confuse themselves with God. It's the kind that realizes God is at work in you, so you can agree with the apostle Paul in Philippians 4:13: "I can do everything through him [Christ] who gives me strength."

Third, *you must be sure it is God's Word that tells you to step out.* Notice that Peter wanted to go out where Jesus was, but before he moved he needed the word from Jesus: "Tell me to come to you." God's Word is our ultimate instruction. Matthew 4:4 gives an account of Jesus' answer to the devil as He was being tempted: "It is written: 'Man does not live on bread [earthly things] alone, *but on every word that comes from the mouth of God.'*" Peter understood that if Jesus gave the word to move, he could trust it.

So Jesus gave Peter one word. "Come!" There are thirty-nine different translations for the word *come* in the New Testament, all of which are action words. God's Word is an action book. As soon as Peter heard and understood the word, he got out of the boat. Peter didn't hesitate. He didn't ask John if they'd laugh at him back in the fisherman's local union hall in Capernaum. He didn't even ask Simon the Zealot if what he was about to do was politically correct. He just got out of the boat.

Should you ever hear God beckoning you to step out in Him, most times you will go alone.

Once out of the boat, Peter didn't just stand there. He started walking. Here he was in a place he had never been before. He found himself walking under circumstances that, before this moment, he would have thought impossible. And the only thing he had to go on was God's word.

But notice that Peter was walking toward Jesus. If your venture "out on the water" does not lead you to Jesus, you're just showing off. Your every step should bring you and others closer to the Lord. The principle is found in Matthew 5:16: "In the same way, let your light shine before men, that they may see your good deeds and praise your Father in heaven." Don't show off for the brothers back in the boat.

Still, Peter was human. One of the hazards of stepping out onto the water is what we can't see beneath us. Matthew 14:30 makes an intriguing point: the water didn't frighten Peter, it was the wind. In other words, participating in the miracle wasn't the problem. The problem for Peter was still in the surrounding circumstances.

We must understand that if God controls the water, He can control the wind as well. The miracle and the circumstances are both fully in His hands. Still, when we need to, we can cry out as did Peter, "Lord, save me!"

If anything goes wrong, Christ is right there to save us. When Peter called out, Jesus immediately reached out His hand and caught him. Jesus is an ever-present help in the time of trouble.

Once you step out, you can even learn from failure. Jesus asked Peter, "You of little faith, why did you doubt?" God wanted Peter to know that even though he had more faith than the brothers on the boat, he still was a doubter at heart. Peter learned humility . . . but he also tasted God's greater potential for him.

If you ever get the call to come out of the boat and do special things for anyone, resolve in your mind to go all the way to Jesus. See it through. Don't let circumstances kill God's calling on your life. Because, as Matthew 14:32 notes, the wind will die down eventually. For the disciples that night, the wind came to test their faith. When the test was over, it left.

God is calling some today to step out into the unknown. He is saying, "I know you've never been here before. But take My Word and learn of Me. I'll show you how to walk on water."

Just like Peter, thousands have stepped out to make a difference in this country. Many of their stories are very seldom told, but the sacrifices they made still speak volumes for them. Allow me to mention a few of the lesser-known examples of everyday heroes who did the unusual for the hope of the miraculous.

Mr. William Lewis Moore, a white postman from Baltimore, was shot and killed on April 23, 1963, as he walked through Attalla, Alabama. Moore was murdered as he staged a one-man march against segregation. He had planned to deliver a letter to the governor of Mississippi urging an end to intolerance. I salute this hero who decided that he had to step out from among the masses and make a difference.

Reverend Bruce Klunder was among civil rights activists who protested the building of a segregated school by placing their bodies in the way of construction equipment. Klunder was crushed to death when a bulldozer backed over him on April 7, 1964.

Reverend James Reeb, another white minister from Boston, was among many clergymen who joined the Selma marchers after the attack of civil rights protesters at the Edmund Pettus Bridge. Reeb was beaten to death by other white men while he walked down a Selma street on March 11, 1965.

And finally, Jonathan Myrick Daniels comes to mind. Daniels was a white Episcopal seminary student, also from Boston. He had come to Alabama to help with the black voter registration in Lowndes County. Daniels was arrested at a demonstration, jailed in Hayneville, and then suddenly released on August 20, 1965. Moments after his release he was shot to death by a deputy sheriff.

The stories could fill many pages of many books. These men and others gave the ultimate sacrifice for people that looked different from them. They are representative of the whites who, just a few decades ago, gave their lives alongside dozens of blacks for the cause of justice.

They leave a rich legacy. But that was then, and this is now. Allow me to suggest how my white brothers and sisters can make a positive difference today, especially in regard to the racial concerns in our Christian family.

The answer is simple: relationships.

Please don't try to be black if you're not. Just be a friend. But understand that to be a friend, you first have to introduce yourself. I have heard countless numbers of Christians say they love everyone. But how can you love someone that you don't know?

First John 4:20 says, "If anyone says, 'I love God,' yet hates his brother, he is a liar. For anyone who does not love his brother, whom he has seen, cannot love God, whom he has not seen." It takes a relationship to love someone. Should you wish to exercise that love, open your heart to God and ask Him to lead you into relationships with Christians of color.

I believe the racial reconciliation movement has much merit. Guided by such giants as John Perkins, people involved in the movement have built many new relationships across racial boundaries. However, I'm not a huge follower of its teachings. To me, reconciliation means renewing a friendship. I find it difficult to renew something I never had. My grandfather didn't have any real friends who were white. My great-great-grandfather was a slave. I doubt the plantation owner was a real good friend of his. To be honest, I can't find anything in my roots that I would want to renew with white folks.

I need a fresh start with them. So my suggestion is that we just meet at the foot of the cross. There we are all truly equal. There we have the ultimate relationship in common: our relationship with our Lord and Savior Jesus Christ. In my experience, I've found that meeting at the cross is the best way to start a relationship on level ground.

Everyone's culture and color are important, and neither should be compromised for the another. When I was growing up *American Bandstand* and *Soul Train* appeared on the same television set. I watched both. If there is room for both of them on commercial television, surely we can find room for both cultures and their peoples within our lives.

Because of Christ we can appreciate the strengths in all cultures. Our churches and organizations can demonstrate to a lost world the example of Christ in many ways. Take partnering, for example. Partnering is just what it sounds like: yoking together to pursue a common purpose. Becoming partners in ministry is a long-term choice. It's this simple: one individual or congregation agrees to share in the labor of another.

Partnering is sharing, not pimping. Over the years, the church has submitted many minority ministry groups to the "puppet style" of assistance. That's when some suburban or evangelical parachuch organization goes to a less prosperous ministry to "help" it along. Unfortunately, most of the time the "help" turned out to be another form of exploitation. The church on the receiving end became little more than a fundraising gimmick for the assisting ministry. Often the inner-city partner was forced to hire or support some person or strategy that didn't work in the neighborhood. Many photographs were taken of underprivileged children and were used to raise funds that the children never saw. Thankfully, this form of evangelical pimping has run its course. The churches it pretended to help don't tolerate it anymore.

Legitimate partnering *empowers* its participants. Through the partnering model churches and their supporters can find fulfillment.

Over the years churches have moved away from the cities and the poor and underprivileged. In fact, we're suffering through a "white flight" situation where I now live. New suburbs keep growing in Colorado that allow folks to segregate themselves, and I suppose that is their right. This is America, after all, and there are some people, both black and white, I don't want to live next door to, either.

Lately, though, it seems the church is taking flight in a way that particularly disturbs me. I call this phenomenon "The Preparing to Go Away with Jesus Movement." Now that things seem to be moving toward more shared leadership in the church, a growing number of evangelicals seem to be stuck on the notion of that one last big move. Heaven seems to be the ultimate "suburb" that countless authors and speakers keep referring to. Please don't misunderstand me. Like all the saints of God, I can't wait to see Jesus in His glory. To fall prostrate before Him and worship Him are my ultimate longings. But if He wants a bride adorned in a dress without spots or wrinkles, I think we'd better try to do some more dry cleaning before He comes.

We have an opportunity to show our Lord how much we loveHim by loving one another today. Let's try.

Before I close, please allow me to kill two roaches with one shoe. There has been much said about the ineffectiveness of the inner-city church in the past twenty-five years. Let me suggest to all those skeptics who feel the church has lost its "urban punch" that there are hundreds of examples of ministry that serve as working models of victorious light.

Here is just one. In Los Angeles, California, the First African Methodist Episcopal Church (or "F.A.M.E.") has the answers its community needs. F.A.M.E. is a shining example of holistic ministry that works in a community many had written off years ago. Pastor Cecil Murray and his congregation have invested and reinvested in the people and property of their neighborhood. Their efforts have given hope and life to thousands who would otherwise have "fallen through the cracks." Even with the emphasis on community and personal development, though, the people of F.A.M.E. have not forgotten the God of our forefathers—they have one of the most joyous church services I have ever experienced.

This congregation and dozens of others should be studied and copied. These churches cross the lines of denominationalism and serve as examples of what can be done when people come together in the name of the Lord to assist a community. I would encourage pastors and ministry leaders who do not have a plan that is working to call, write, or drop in on the ministry in your city that is making a difference. And I trust that you brothers and sisters who have it together will continue to share your recipes for success. We need to help each other step out in faith.

As for me, I plan to continue my journey. I have no idea when it will end or where the road will take me. Should life refuse me a comfortable, clean, shiny form of transportation for my journey, that's all right. I've learned over the years that no matter how I travel, the important thing is to keep moving, whether it's through a messed-up ride or a dressed-up walk.

Postscript

NOW YOU KNOW why I'm so committed to young people. I've dedicated my life and work to the next generation of Americans who will someday take our places in society.

You, too, can commit to the lives and development of America's children by becoming a USA Child Share Partner through Compassion International. Your financial commitment can be part of the solution to the problems that face today's youth. Call Compassion at 1 (800) 336–7676 for more information, or write: Compassion International, P.O. Box 7000, Colorado Springs, CO 80933.

It is my greatest wish that my life serve as an example to you of God's love. Like you, I have had many bumps and sharp curves to master. Yet I pray that my story has encouraged you to stay in the race and complete your course. And should you come across some soul along the way whose ride is broken down, perhaps you could find the time to give that soul a jump start.

Until He comes,
Jerald